THE LATER NEW TESTAMENT WRITINGS AND SCRIPTURE

THE LATER NEW TESTAMENT WRITINGS AND SCRIPTURE

The Old Testament *in* Acts, Hebrews, the Catholic Epistles and Revelation

STEVE MOYISE

Baker Academic
a division of Baker Publishing Group
Grand Rapids, Michigan

Published in 2012 by Baker Academic
a division of Baker Publishing Group
P.O. Box 6287, Grand Rapids, MI 49516-6287
www.bakeracademic.com

Originally published in 2012 as *The Later New Testament Writers and Scripture:
The Old Testament in Acts, Hebrews, the Catholic Epistles and Revelation* by
Society for Promoting Christian Knowledge, London, United Kingdom

Printed in the United States of America

Library of Congress Cataloging-in-Publication data is on file at the Library
of Congress, Washington, DC.

ISBN 978-0-8010-4853-1

The internet addresses, email addresses, and phone numbers in this book
are accurate at the time of publication. They are provided as a resource.
Baker Publishing Group does not endorse them or vouch for their
content or permanence.

12 13 14 15 16 17 18   7 6 5 4 3 2 1

Contents

Contents

Contents

Acknowledgements

Unless otherwise noted, Scripture quotations (sometimes marked NRSV) are from the New Revised Standard Version of the Bible, Anglicized Edition, copyright © 1989, 1995 by the Division of Christian Education of the National Council of the Churches of Christ in the USA. Used by permission. All rights reserved.

Quotations marked KJV are from the Authorized Version of the Bible (The King James Bible), the rights in which are vested in the Crown, and are reproduced by permission of the Crown's Patentee, Cambridge University Press.

Quotations marked NAB are from the *New American Bible with Revised New Testament and Revised Psalms*, are copyright © 1991, 1986, 1970 Confraternity of Christian Doctrine, Washington, D.C. and are used by permission of the copyright owner. All rights reserved.

Quotations marked NEB are from the New English Bible, copyright © The Delegates of the Oxford University Press and The Syndics of Cambridge University Press, 1961, 1970. Used by permission.

Quotations marked NIV are from the HOLY BIBLE, NEW INTERNATIONAL VERSION. Copyright © 1973, 1978, 1984 by International Bible Society. Used by permission of Hodder & Stoughton Publishers, a member of the Hachette UK Group. All rights reserved. 'NIV' is a registered trademark of International Bible Society. UK trademark number 1448790.

Quotations marked NJB are from The New Jerusalem Bible, published and copyright © 1985 by Darton, Longman & Todd Ltd and Doubleday & Co., Inc., a division of Random House, Inc. and used by permission.

Quotations marked REB are from the Revised English Bible, copyright © Oxford University Press and Cambridge University Press 1989.

Acknowledgements

Quotations marked RSV are from the Revised Standard Version of the Bible, copyright © 1946, 1952 and 1971 by the Division of Christian Education of the National Council of the Churches of Christ in the USA. Used by permission. All rights reserved.

Abbreviations

AB	Anchor Bible
BECNT	Baker Exegetical Commentary on the New Testament
ICC	International Critical Commentary
JSNT	*Journal for the Study of the New Testament*
JSNTSup	*Journal for the Study of the New Testament, Supplement Series*
JTS	*Journal of Theological Studies*
LHB	Library of Hebrew Studies
LNTS	Library of New Testament Studies
LXX	Septuagint (Greek translation)
MT	Masoretic Text (standard version of the Hebrew Bible)
NA	Nestle-Aland, *Novum Testamentum Graece*, 27th edition
NICNT	The New International Commentary on the New Testament
NIGTC	The New International Greek Testament Commentary
PNTC	Pillar New Testament Commentary
SNTSM	Society for New Testament Studies Monograph Series
UBS	United Bible Society, *Greek New Testament*, 4th edition
WBC	Word Biblical Commentary
WUNT	Wissenschaftliche Untersuchungen zum Neuen Testament

Introduction

In the two previous volumes, we used the Gospels – mainly Matthew, Mark and Luke – to reconstruct *Jesus and Scripture* and Paul's letters – mainly Romans, Galatians, 1 and 2 Corinthians – to give an account of *Paul and Scripture*.[1] In this volume, we consider the use of Scripture in the rest of the New Testament and following the pattern of the InterVarsity series of Bible Dictionaries,[2] we have given it the title, *The Later New Testament Writings and Scripture*. Here we find important engagements with Scripture by the authors of Acts, Hebrews and Revelation, as well as the shorter works of James, 1 and 2 Peter, 1, 2 and 3 John and Jude. Some of these works may well be earlier than some of the Gospels but in general, they represent what came after Jesus and Paul – hence the title. As we shall see, they show that texts used by Jesus (Gen. 2; Lev. 19; Exod. 20; Pss. 22, 110, 118; Isa. 6) and Paul (Gen. 3; Deut. 32; Pss. 2, 8; Isa. 8, 28, 40, 52—53; Hab. 2) continued to be important, while new texts, such as Psalm 16 (Acts), Psalm 95 (Heb.) and Ezekiel 1—3 (Rev.) were explored.

We will begin our study with the Acts of the Apostles. Here we face the same question as in our study of the Gospels: are we reading the views of the author – traditionally known as Luke – or the various characters in the story? There are three main answers to this question. The first assumes that Luke was a serious historian who had access to notes and summaries of the events he narrated (cf. Luke 1.1–4). This does not mean that we have the actual words of the apostles for, at the very least, those preaching in Jerusalem would have spoken in Aramaic and quoted Scripture either in Hebrew or one of its Aramaic translations. Since Luke wrote in Greek, he either translated the Aramaic speeches for himself or depended on sources that had already done so. This raises an important question concerning the biblical quotations in the speeches: do they represent a translation of what was actually said or are they quotations from the Greek version of the Bible, known as the Septuagint or LXX? As we shall see, the latter is more likely but, even with such a caveat, those who hold to this first view consider the speeches of Acts to be an accurate representation of what was actually said.

The opposite view is that the speeches were constructed by Luke as a means of communicating his own beliefs and interests. They do not represent what the early apostles said but are a result of many years of theological reflection. One of the main arguments for this view is that Peter's Pentecost sermon in Jerusalem (Acts 2) is very similar to Paul's synagogue sermon in Antioch (Acts 13), whereas we know from Galatians 2 that Peter and Paul had very different ministries. It is also difficult to imagine that James made his point at the so-called Jerusalem council (Acts 15) by citing a peculiarity of the LXX version of Amos 9.11–12 (see p. 11). This has convinced some scholars that what we have in Acts bears little relationship to what was actually said but is the product of many decades of theological reflection. This would not be a problem for our study for we are investigating the later writings of the New Testament. However, other scholars have noted that the early speeches appear to contain some 'primitive' elements and so a third view is that, in common with other historians of the time, what we have in Acts is not a transcript of what was said but what Luke considered to be 'typical' of the sort of thing that the apostles would have said.

We will not try and answer this question in advance but it will be instructive to follow our study of Acts with a study of the letters of Peter, since the first half of Acts is dominated by Peter's speeches. Such a comparison is not as straightforward as it might seem since there is considerable debate about the authorship of 1 and 2 Peter. Most scholars find it hard to accept that the two letters were written by the same person – as did many in the first few centuries of the Church – and some suggest that Peter was not directly responsible for writing 1 Peter, perhaps allowing his secretary (1 Pet. 5.12) a major role in its composition. Nevertheless, such a comparison remains instructive for, at the very least, we will be comparing the speeches of 'Peter' as recorded in Acts with the teaching of 'Peter' as recorded in 1 Peter. It turns out that in Acts, the major influence in Peter's speeches is the Psalms, supported by a few references to Isaiah, while in 1 Peter, it is Isaiah supported by a few references to the Psalms. Whether this is significant for the question of authorship will be discussed at the end of that chapter.

Because of the huge differences between 1 and 2 Peter, a separate chapter will be devoted to 2 Peter, along with the very similar letter of Jude. The two letters share some striking verbal parallels and most scholars think that 2 Peter has used Jude as one of his sources. Both letters show a marked interest in angels and demons and draw on apocryphal stories such as the flood being caused by fallen angels (Jude 6; 2 Pet. 2.4). Indeed, the only explicit quotation in Jude is taken from *1 Enoch* (Jude 14–15), a work that was very popular among the Qumran community but not included in the canon of Scripture. We include in this chapter a study of James, which has also been treated as idiosyncratic because of its use of the same text that Paul uses (Gen. 15.6) to argue that 'a person is justified by works and *not by faith alone*' (Jas. 2.24). As is well known, Martin Luther had great problems with this letter though most scholars today have a more positive attitude towards it.

The next two chapters consider the important and original engagement with Scripture found in Hebrews and Revelation. Hebrews begins with a catena ('chain') of quotations to demonstrate Christ's superiority to angels (Heb. 1.5–12) and continues to demonstrate his superiority over Moses, Aaron and the whole Levitical priesthood. Drawing on Psalm 110.4, the author argues that Jesus belongs to the priesthood of Melchizedek and uses the story of Abraham giving gifts to King Melchizedek in Genesis 14 to support it. Scholars have found it difficult to characterize the author's use of Scripture. It has a number of traditional traits, such as the use of Psalms 2, 22, 110 and 118, but also has parallels with Qumran (a text about Melchizedek was found there), Philo (earthly realities are shadows of heavenly realities) and the rabbis (many of the exegetical techniques are the same).

Revelation also represents a creative development but in a rather different direction. There are no explicit quotations in Revelation but its visionary descriptions are almost entirely composed of biblical phrases. Thus the risen Christ, who is described with considerable restraint in the Gospels, has eyes 'like a flame of fire', hair as 'white as snow', feet 'like burnished bronze' and a voice 'like the sound of many waters' (Rev. 1.14–16). These descriptions are drawn from Old Testament visions of God (Dan. 7; Ezek. 43) and angels (Dan. 10), as are the visions of judgement and salvation that fill the rest of the book. This raises the intriguing question of whether the seer of these visions effectively saw what Daniel and Ezekiel saw or is using Old Testament imagery to evoke the theological ideas that he wished to communicate.

As explained in the previous volumes, the quotations found in the New Testament seldom agree exactly with the wording found in modern English Bibles and there are a number of reasons for this. First, the New Testament authors generally quote from a Greek translation rather than the Hebrew text, upon which an English Bible depends. This inevitably leads to differences in wording, just as no two English Bibles are the same. Second, in some cases the New Testament authors appear to know a version of the text that differs from the majority of manuscripts that have come down to us. The discovery of the Dead Sea Scrolls (1948–) has shown that the biblical text existed in several forms in the first century and it is not always clear which form is being quoted. Third, it was sometimes necessary for the New Testament authors to modify the text to make it fit the grammar and syntax of the new sentence. Indeed, on some occasions, it appears that modifications were made in order to make the quotation better fit the argument, a practice that is surprising to the modern reader but is well attested in the ancient world. When these differences are a matter of debate among scholars, the relevant details can be found in the endnotes. As a starting point to our investigations, we will draw on the list of quotations found in *The Greek New Testament*, published by the United Bible Societies (see Appendix).

It should also be noted that the study of allusions and echoes has been a significant feature in recent debate and is by no means confined to the book of Revelation. Allusions are by definition elusive but can be of great significance if they evoke major themes in Scripture, such as exodus, covenant or exile. We will see that a number of scholars think that 'return from exile' is a significant theme in the New Testament writings, though there is debate as to whether it is best described as an 'influence' on the author or a 'framework' that guided the composition. Since there are hundreds of allusions cited in UBS and even more in the Nestle-Aland version of the Greek New Testament (NA), we will only have space to mention some of the more prominent ones in this book. For more detailed study, readers are referred to the endnotes that accompany each chapter.

The Gospels

Although we have used the sayings of Jesus found in the four Gospels to reconstruct *Jesus and Scripture*, the Gospels themselves properly belong to this volume, since they were written after Paul's letters (Mark is probably the earliest from about 65–70 CE). They have not been included here for two reasons. First, it would have involved a great deal of repetition for most of the quotations in the Gospels (with the exception of Matthew) are on the lips of Jesus and have already been discussed. Second, I have already covered this material in Chapters 2–5 of my book, *The Old Testament in the New*,[3] which again would have led to much repetition. We will of course be discussing Luke, though our focus will be on Acts rather than the Gospel.

1

Acts and Scripture

Introduction

There are around 40 explicit quotations of Scripture in Acts (see Appendix), most of which occur in the long speech of Stephen in Acts 7 (15), the various speeches of Peter in Acts 1—4 (14) and Paul's speeches in Acts 13, 23 and 28 (9). In addition, there is a quotation from James in the so-called Jerusalem council of Acts 15 and an editorial comment in Acts 8 that the Ethiopian eunuch was reading from Isaiah 53.7–8 when Philip joined him in his chariot. The quotations are drawn from the Pentateuch (19), Historical books (1), Prophets (9) and Psalms (11), although the distribution is uneven, since 13 of the quotations from the Pentateuch occur in Stephen's long summary of Israel's history. Peter's speeches are dominated by the Psalms (2, 16, 69, 109, 110, 118, 132), with only one quotation from the Prophets (Joel). Paul's speeches show an equal interest in Psalms (2, 16, 89) and Prophets (Isa. 6, 49, 55; Hab. 1), with one quotation from the Pentateuch (Exod. 22.28) and one from the Historical books (1 Sam. 13.14). After Stephen's long summary of Israel's history, he makes his point about sacrifices and the temple by quoting from Amos 5.25–27 and Isaiah 66.1–2, while James argues for the inclusion of the Gentiles from Amos 9.11–12.

The majority of scholars believe that Acts is the sequel to Luke's Gospel (cf. Acts 1.1 and Luke 1.1–4) and this raises an important question about our enquiry. Should the material in Luke's Gospel inform our study of 'Acts and Scripture' or should we study the book in its own right? Our decision is a pragmatic one, since much of the material in Luke's Gospel has already been discussed in *Jesus and Scripture*, and so our primary focus will be on Acts alone. However, it should be noted that some scholars believe that the material in Luke's Gospel significantly changes how the material in Acts should be viewed and we will consider such views towards the end of this chapter.

The other major question for our study is the relationship between the speeches and the narratives of Acts. Since all but one of the quotations occurs in the speeches, a study that confines itself to the quotations is a study that confines itself to the speeches. These are clearly important to Luke and one of the main vehicles for conveying his theological convictions, but we should remember that they do only constitute one third of the material. There are many allusions and echoes to Scripture in other parts of Acts, as well as important summaries of scriptural material. Space does not permit a full study of these but in our final section on 'Major interpretations of Acts and Scripture', we will see how some of them have been significant in shaping particular theories of Luke's use of Scripture.

There would be considerable merit in now working through the scriptural material in order but it would result in a very long study and also be very easy to miss the wood for the trees. We will therefore begin with a thematic study, looking at how the quotations are used to support the following themes: salvation for Jews and Gentiles; Christ's death, resurrection and exaltation; christological titles and functions; judgement; and historical summary. We will then consider some key texts in the narrative portions of Acts before looking at a number of scholarly proposals for understanding 'Acts and Scripture', including those that include Luke's Gospel. We begin with a theme that is crucial for Luke and his readers, namely, that salvation is for Jews and Gentiles.[1]

Salvation for Jews and Gentiles

The book of Acts opens with Jesus instructing his disciples to wait in Jerusalem until the Holy Spirit empowers them to witness 'in Jerusalem, in all Judea and Samaria, and to the ends of the earth' (Acts 1.8). The treachery of Judas is still in their thoughts and Peter urges them to choose a replacement, quoting snippets from Psalm 69.25 and 109.8 in the form: '"Let his homestead become desolate, and let there be no one to live in it"; and "Let another take his position of overseer."' The process is interesting (Acts 1.21–26). First, a condition is set: it must be someone who has been with them from the beginning, and two men, Joseph and Matthias, meet the requirements. Second, the disciples pray that God, who knows everyone's heart (Ps. 44.21), should make it clear which one has been chosen. And third, following ancient biblical practices (Lev. 16.8; Josh. 18.6; Neh. 11.1), they cast lots and the lot falls to Matthias. One might have expected such a momentous decision to have awaited the coming of the Holy Spirit and it is interesting that Matthias is never mentioned again. However, perhaps it was more important that 'the twelve' were complete when the day of Pentecost arrived.

When that day came, there was a 'sound like the rush of a violent wind' and 'tongues, as of fire' settled upon each of them. They were 'filled with the Holy Spirit and began to speak in other languages' (Acts 2.1–4). The crowd were amazed that they were hearing the message in their own language but some sneered and accused them of being drunk. Peter refutes this, stating that they could hardly be drunk at nine in the morning (times have changed!); rather, what they are seeing and hearing are the signs of the 'last days' as prophesied by the prophet Joel.[2] There follows a long quotation of Joel 2.28–32, which speaks of God pouring out his Spirit upon all people, cosmic signs (sun turned to darkness, moon to blood) and the promise that 'everyone who calls on the name of the Lord shall be saved' (Acts 2.21). The speech that follows focuses on Jesus' death and resurrection (discussed below) but it ends with the promise that through repentance and baptism, they too can receive the Holy Spirit and this promise is 'for your children, and for all who are far away, everyone whom the Lord our God calls to him' (Acts 2.39).

Despite the universal sounding language ('everyone who calls'), Joel was referring to those in Judah and Jerusalem, not the Gentiles, who could only look forward to judgement (Joel 3.1–16).[3] And this may indeed be Peter's meaning, for the narrative that follows shows considerable reluctance to preach to non-Jews. The same could be said of Peter's second recorded speech (Acts 3.12–26), where the promise of Genesis 22.18/26.4 ('by your offspring shall all the nations of the earth be blessed/gain blessing'[4]) is quoted. Paul would have no trouble applying such texts to the Gentile mission (Gal. 3.6–9) but two things stand in the way of such an interpretation here. First, Peter refers to his hearers as those who are 'descendants of the prophets and of the covenant that God gave to your ancestors' (Acts 3.25), which sounds like a reference to Jews. Second, the form of the quotation in Acts speaks of 'all families' rather than 'all nations', which could be a deliberate change in order to maintain the application to Jews. On the other hand, the speech says that Jesus 'must remain in heaven until the time of universal restoration that God announced long ago through his holy prophets' (Acts 3.21). The phrase 'universal restoration' is literally 'times of restoration of all things', which sounds like a reference to all people, though it could also mean 'all God's plans for Israel'.

Such ambiguity is removed when we get to Paul's speech in the synagogue at Pisidian Antioch (Acts 13). The speech rehearses Israel's early history and then jumps to the death and resurrection of Jesus. Many are convinced but some Jews reject the message, prompting the statement: 'It was necessary that the word of God should be spoken first to you. Since you reject it and judge yourselves to be unworthy of eternal life, we are now turning to the Gentiles' (Acts 13.46). This action is then supported by a quotation from Isaiah 49.6b: 'I will give you as a light to the nations, that my salvation may reach to the end of the earth.' The passage is apt in that it speaks of the servant's mission to Israel, which expands into a mission to the nations, and there may even be a hint that the former is being frustrated ('I have laboured in vain, I have spent my strength for nothing and vanity' – Isa. 49.4). However, one would have expected the title 'light to the nations' to be applied to Jesus rather than Paul and Barnabas, as indeed it is in Acts 26.23–24, where Paul says to Festus:

> To this day I have had help from God, and so I stand here, testifying to both small and great, saying nothing but what the prophets and Moses said would take place: that the Messiah must suffer, and that, by being the first to rise from the dead, he would proclaim *light* both to our people and *to the Gentiles*.
>
> (Acts 26.22–24)

The solution is probably to be found in the Isaiah passage itself, which oscillates between a corporate reference ('You are my servant, Israel, in whom I will be glorified' – Isa. 49.3) and an individual reference ('The LORD called me before I was born' – Isa. 49.1). In a similar way, Jesus' role as 'light to the nations' carries over to those who proclaim him, since it is that very proclamation that fulfils the commission: 'By virtue of the church's relationship to Christ, and because the promises fulfilled in him are also fulfilled in and through his church, when the servant-Messiah received Yahweh's commission to be light to the nations, so did the church'.[5] It is also of note that the phrase 'spoken *first to you*' reminds the reader of the final words of Peter's speech in Acts 3.26 ('When God raised up his servant, he sent him *first to you*'). Nothing is said of a Gentile mission in those first two speeches but we now learn that 'first to you' carried an implication – then to the nations.

The fourth passage to be considered is attributed to James during the so-called Jerusalem council and seeks to establish that a mission to the Gentiles was endorsed by the whole Church. After much debate (Acts 15.7), Peter describes his experience of preaching to Gentiles, followed by Paul and Barnabas. James then brings things to a conclusion by claiming that this 'agrees with the words of the prophets', followed by a quotation from Amos 9.11–12:

> After this I will return, and I will rebuild the dwelling of David, which has fallen; I will rebuild its ruins, and I will set it up, that the *rest of men* may *seek* the Lord, and all the Gentiles who are called by my name, says the Lord, who has made these things known from of old. (Acts 15.16–18 RSV)

As quoted, the text declares that God's intent has always been to restore Israel ('rebuild the dwelling of David') and bring in the Gentiles. As such, it offers an important scriptural warrant for the rest of the narrative, where Paul will take the gospel to Athens, the intellectual capital of the world (Acts 17), and Rome, the political centre (Acts 28). However, a surprise is in store for readers who look up the passage in Amos, for the Hebrew text – which lies behind our English versions – says that God will raise up the dwelling of David 'in order that they may *possess* the remnant of *Edom* and all the nations who are called by my name' (Amos 9.12). Now it could be that the Greek was translating a different Hebrew text to the one that has come down to us, but most scholars are struck by the fact that the two major differences – the change in verb from 'possess' to 'seek' and the change in noun from 'Edom' to 'men/humanity' – only differ by a single letter in Hebrew. Whether by design or mistake, it was then necessary to make the phrase 'rest of men' the subject of the verb 'seek' instead of the object of the verb 'possess'. The result is a text which emphasizes the full inclusion of the Gentiles, rather than their subjugation.[6]

In reading these four episodes, the question naturally arises: Is Luke's understanding different from that of the characters in the story? With Peter's speeches in Acts 2 and 3, the issue is not so much about the difference between the Greek and Hebrew texts but the different contexts: Peter is preaching to

Jews in Jerusalem and Luke is writing to Gentiles like Theophilus. The latter is likely to have taken phrases like 'everyone who calls', 'all families' and 'restores all things' as references to Gentiles like himself but are we to imagine that Peter's hearers in Jerusalem would have done so? Similarly, Theophilus would undoubtedly have taken the quotation of Amos 9.11–12 LXX to mean that God has always intended to call Gentiles, but can we imagine James settling a dispute in Jerusalem by citing a Greek text that differs markedly from its Hebrew counterpart? Would not those who were insisting that Gentile Christians should keep the law (Acts 15.1) have pointed out that the Hebrew text of Amos 9.11–12 speaks of the 'subjugation' of the Gentiles, surely carrying the implication that they should be instructed to keep Israel's law?[7]

The issue is not what Peter or James originally meant for we have no way of knowing whether they said anything like this at all. It is more a debate about what Luke wanted Theophilus to deduce from these speeches. Did he want him to assume that Peter and James would have meant the same thing that he, as a Gentile, would have understood by these texts? Or was he expecting a little more sophistication; that texts that were ambiguous when quoted in Jerusalem have become clear now that the gospel has been preached to the Gentiles? It is not a question we can answer at this stage but what we can say is that one of Luke's uses of Scripture is to progressively reveal that God has always intended to save Gentiles as well as Jews.

Christ's death, resurrection and exaltation

Christ's death

Despite the frequent summaries that Scripture foretold the suffering of Christ, very few texts are actually cited to that effect. The two clearest are Psalm 118.22, quoted in the form, 'the stone that was rejected by you, the builders' (Acts 4.11), and Isaiah

53.7–8 ('Like a sheep he was led to the slaughter . . . his life is taken away from the earth') in Acts 8.32–33. The first belongs to Peter's fourth speech where he indicts the rulers and elders of Jerusalem for crucifying Jesus. This was not the end of the matter, however, for God raised him from the dead, and thus Jesus is 'the stone that was rejected by you, the builders; it has become the cornerstone' (Acts 4.11). Luke has already recorded Jesus quoting this text at the conclusion to the parable of the vineyard (Luke 20.17), where it agrees with the LXX. Here, it has been modified to address the rulers and elders directly ('by you, the builders') and sharpened by changing the verb from 'rejected' to 'despised'. This is not clear in the NRSV but in Luke's other two uses of the same verb (Luke 18.9; 23.11), NRSV uses the word 'contempt' on both occasions. As Barrett notes, one might reject a stone for being unsuitable but one hardly regards it with contempt. The change in verb is because Jesus is now associated with the stone and tradition records that he was indeed treated with contempt, as Luke has already recorded (Luke 23.11).[8]

The quotation indicates that Jesus would suffer contempt but it does not specifically say that he would die or offer any insights into the meaning of his death. The quotation of Isaiah 53.7–8 in Acts 8.32–33 looks more promising. Philip is told by an angel to meet a court official returning home to Ethiopia after worshipping in Jerusalem. The man is in his chariot reading from the prophet Isaiah and Luke cites the passage that has him puzzled: 'Like a sheep he was led to the slaughter, and like a lamb silent before its shearer, so he does not open his mouth. In his humiliation justice was denied him. Who can describe his generation? For his life is taken away from the earth' (Acts 8.32–33).

The man asks Philip the obvious question: 'About whom, may I ask you, does the prophet say this, about himself or about someone else?' (Acts 8.34). We are not told Philip's answer but given a summary statement that 'starting with this scripture, he proclaimed to him the good news about Jesus' (Acts 8.35). What is it that Luke wishes Theophilus to deduce from this? The quoted text makes two points: his death was unjust and he offered no resistance. Some think the word 'slaughter' implies that the death was a sacrifice but the parallel reference to 'shearing' counts against this, and 'sheep for slaughter' was a common metaphor for sudden death (Ps. 44.11; Jer. 12.3; Zech. 11.7 – see also Rom. 8.36). The key then appears to lie in the meaning of the phrase 'starting with this scripture'. Are we to understand that Philip went on to expound the rest of the fourth servant song (Isa. 52.13—53.12) and if so, to what effect? He could have focused on phrases like 'he shall bear their iniquities' (53.11) and 'he bore the sin of many' (53.12) to offer an explanation for Jesus' death. Or he could have focused on the positive statements in 53.11 ('Out of his anguish he shall see light') and 53.12 ('I will allot him a portion with the great') in order to speak about his vindication.

On the other hand, Luke has already said something similar at the end of his Gospel, where Jesus 'began' (same Greek word) with Moses and the prophets and 'interpreted to them the things about himself in all the scriptures' (Luke 24.27). This might suggest that Philip did likewise, moving from the quoted text to other Scriptures – most naturally those already quoted in Luke–Acts – to speak about Jesus' death and resurrection. If this is the case, then the emphasis is not so much on the meaning of Jesus' death but the divine necessity for all the major facets of Jesus' life, death and resurrection. This then would be the good news that Philip preached to the Ethiopian and caused him to request an immediate baptism.

These are the only two quotations that focus on Jesus' death and neither is explicitly about its meaning. There is also a possible allusion when it is said that Jesus was put to death by 'hanging him on a tree' (Acts 5.30; 10.39; see also 13.29). For readers of the New Testament, this sounds like Paul's reference to Deuteronomy 21.23 in Galatians 3.13 ('Christ redeemed us from the curse of the law by becoming a curse for us – for it is written, "Cursed is everyone who hangs on a tree"'). But what would Theophilus have understood by the phrase? He would know that Jesus died on a Roman cross, so that the mention of 'tree' might prompt further thought, and eventually lead to the Deuteronomy text. On the other hand, these passages in Acts could be taken as evidence that Jesus dying on a tree was simply part of the received tradition and it is the specific situation in Galatia that prompted Paul to make theological capital out of it. If we deduce from Luke 1.1–4 that Theophilus had only received a cursory account of Christianity, then it is perhaps more likely that he would not have seen a deeper meaning in the reference to 'tree'. Thus in conclusion, although it is important for Luke that Jesus' death was 'according to Scripture', he does not use specific texts to elaborate on its meaning.

Christ's resurrection

In Peter's Pentecost speech, he accuses his hearers of crucifying Jesus 'by the hands of those outside the law' (Acts 2.23), but the good news is that God raised him up 'because it was impossible for him to be held in its power' (Acts 2.24). Peter's scriptural support for this comes from Psalm 16, where David expresses his confidence in God in such expressions as 'I have a goodly heritage' (v. 6), 'because he is at my right hand, I shall not be moved' (v. 8) and 'my body also rests secure' (v. 9). However, it is David's confidence that God will protect him from death in v. 10 that is the subject of Peter's exposition. Peter cites the text in the form: 'For you will not abandon my soul to Hades, or let your Holy One experience corruption' (Acts 2.27). He then argues that David did in fact die and so this could not be a reference to himself. Rather, he spoke as a prophet and knowing that God 'would put one of his descendants on his throne . . . spoke of the resurrection of the Messiah' (Acts 2.30–31).

As with James's quotation from Amos, the interpretation appears to be facilitated by the particular LXX translation. According to the NRSV, the Hebrew reads: 'For you do not give me up to Sheol, or let your faithful one see the Pit' (Ps. 16.10). The Hebrew parallelism suggests that 'me' and 'faithful one' refer to the same person, and 'Sheol' and 'Pit' refer to the same fate. In other words, David is expressing his confidence that despite his present distress, he does not believe that it will end in his death. Peter's announcement that David did in fact die would hardly have caused his hearers to question the passage, for they would know from Scripture that David died in old age, having reigned in Israel for 40 years (1 Kings 2.10–12). The point of Psalm 16.10 is that God would protect him from death *on this occasion*. However, the LXX lends itself to a different interpretation by speaking of God not abandoning 'my soul to Hades' or allowing 'your Holy One [to] experience corruption'. Each of the translation choices (soul, Hades, Holy One, corruption) can be defended[9] but the combined effect is to shift the meaning from 'avoiding death' to 'surviving death'. Thus when Peter asserts that David died, he can suggest that David – who was known to be a prophet – must have been speaking of someone who would survive death, namely God's 'Holy One', the Messiah.

Interestingly, the argument is repeated in Paul's speech at Pisidian Antioch but it is much clearer because he omits the personal reference to David ('For you will not abandon *my soul* to Hades'), leaving only the reference to God's 'Holy One':

> As to his raising him from the dead, no more to return to corruption, he has spoken in this way, 'I will give you the holy promises made to David.' Therefore he has also said in another psalm, '*You will not let your Holy One experience corruption.*' For David, after he had served the purpose of God in his own generation, died, was laid beside his ancestors, and experienced corruption; but he whom God raised up experienced no corruption. (Acts 13.34–37)

However, Paul adds a complication of his own because the phrase from Isaiah 55.3 ('I will give *you* the holy promises made to David') cannot refer to Jesus as the word 'you' is plural. The meaning must be that Paul's hearers have received the 'holy promises made to David' by virtue of Christ's resurrection from the dead, which is then confirmed by Psalm 16.10.

Finally, although the personal reference to 'my soul' is omitted in Paul's use of the text – perhaps because Luke perceived the difficulty – how are we to understand it in Peter's speech? Is it a case of *sensus plenior*, that David said more than he knew? David thought he was talking about himself but the Holy Spirit, who inspired the words, was referring to Christ? Or is it that David's prophetic gift not only allowed him to speak *about* the Messiah but on occasions, allowed him to speak *for* the Messiah? In other words, Peter's argument is not that these words of David can be typologically applied to the Messiah; it is that this was actually the Messiah speaking through David.

Typological interpretation

The Greek word *typos* means 'pattern' or 'example' (Acts 7.44) but following Paul's use of the term to describe Adam as a 'type' of Christ (Rom. 5.14), it gave rise to a form of interpretation where certain Old Testament events, objects or people were said to 'prefigure' what occurs in the New Testament. Its importance lies in its difference from two other modes of interpretation, namely fulfilment and allegory. Many things in the New Testament are said to be a fulfilment of Scripture but when the original text is identified, it does not contain any explicit promise about the future. This was said to be a typological fulfilment rather than a literal one. On the other hand, allegorical interpretation as practised by people like Philo, finds symbolic meaning in texts that has little to do with their original meaning. Typological interpretation seeks to avoid this by insisting that there must be a very real correspondence between the original and its counterpart.[10]

Christ's exaltation

Luke ends his Gospel with a brief description of Jesus' ascension to heaven (Luke 24.50–53), seemingly on the evening of Easter Sunday, which is then retold in Acts 1.9–11, where it is said to have occurred 40 days after the resurrection. When the day of Pentecost comes (50 days after Passover), Peter's citation of Joel implies that it is God who has poured out the Holy Spirit but, later in the speech, Peter asserts that Jesus has been 'exalted at the right hand of God' and has 'poured out this that you both see and hear' (Acts 2.33). The scriptural support for the ascension/exaltation of Jesus comes from Psalm 110.1: 'For David did not ascend into the heavens, but he himself says, "The Lord said to my Lord, 'Sit at my right hand, until I make your enemies your footstool'"' (Acts 2.34–35).

Peter has already asserted that David did not escape death and now he says that he did not ascend to heaven. It carries the same implication – that he must be speaking about someone else and that person is designated in the psalm as 'my Lord'. The honorific title suggests someone who is superior to King David and Peter deduces that this someone can only be the Messiah. The text is quoted by Jesus in the Gospels and scholars are divided as to whether this explains Peter's usage here or whether Peter's (Luke's) usage explains how the words came to be on Jesus' lips.[11] The former seems more likely since the quotation in the Gospels is left as a puzzle: Jesus asks the scribes how the Messiah can be both the 'son of David' and David's Lord (Luke 20.41–44). There is no suggestion in the story that Jesus is claiming to be this figure. However, the puzzle is solved in Acts 2.34–35 when Jesus is identified as David's Lord, and hence the dialogue in the psalm is between God and Jesus.

The statement that Jesus is at God's right hand is also affirmed in Peter's fourth speech ('God exalted him at his right hand as Leader and Saviour') with the interesting consequence: 'that he might give repentance to Israel and forgiveness of sins' (Acts

5.31). Luke does not focus on the death of Christ as the *means* of forgiveness, as other New Testament writers do (Rom. 5.10; Heb. 10.12; 1 Pet. 2.24; Rev. 5.9). It is his exaltation to the right hand of God that allows him to pour out the Spirit (Acts 2.33) which leads to the offer of forgiveness.

Jesus' position in heaven is further affirmed in Stephen's speech where shortly before he dies, he sees 'the glory of God and Jesus *standing* at the right hand of God' (Acts 7.55). Although the language of 'standing' and 'sitting' is not to be taken literally, it is nevertheless interesting that Luke decides to change it on this occasion. One suggestion is that by standing, Jesus is getting ready to welcome Stephen to heaven. What is clear is that it is important to Luke that Jesus ascended to heaven and Psalm 110.1 is his key text to support it. As with his use of Psalm 16, the argument is that David could not have been speaking about himself but was speaking as a prophet.

Christological titles and functions

Lord and Messiah

In providing support for Jesus' resurrection and ascension, Luke has used the Psalms to demonstrate that David was speaking about the Messiah, which he then identifies as Jesus: 'Therefore let the entire house of Israel know with certainty that God has made him both Lord and Messiah, this Jesus whom you crucified' (Acts 2.36). Not surprisingly, there has been much debate as to the precise meaning of the word 'made' (*epoiēsan*) in this statement. It appears to suggest that Jesus was *not* Lord and Messiah during his earthly life but only *became* those things at his resurrection/ascension (see Rom. 1.3–4). This is different to later writings where Jesus was one with God from the beginning (John 1.1–18), but it is quite plausible on Peter's lips. Some have argued that texts like Luke 1.43 ('And why has this happened to me, that the mother of my *Lord* comes to me?') and Luke 2.11 ('to you is born this day in the city of David a Saviour, who is the *Messiah*, the *Lord*') show that Luke thinks these titles were applicable to Jesus throughout his life. They would thus understand Acts 2.36 as God's confirmation of Jesus' status rather than the bestowal of something new. However, this is not really the point. Luke might have thought that Jesus was Lord and Messiah throughout his life but the question is whether he wants to portray Peter as expounding such views in his very first speech. Barrett thinks not, arguing that the verb translated 'made' does not easily shift to 'confirmed' and so Peter's statement is best regarded as expressing an 'unreflective' theology rather than a mistaken one.[12]

Further support for Jesus' messiahship comes from Psalm 2, which is collectively quoted by the disciples to explain why the great and mighty opposed Jesus and why they continue to oppose his servants:

> Sovereign Lord, who made the heaven and the earth, the sea, and everything in them, it is you who said by the Holy Spirit through our ancestor David, your servant: 'Why did the Gentiles rage, and the peoples imagine vain things? The kings of the earth took their stand, and the rulers have gathered together against the Lord and against his Messiah [lit. "anointed"].'
>
> (Acts 4.24–26)

Though the 'decoding' is not precise, the 'Gentiles', 'peoples' and 'kings' of the psalm are equated with the various groups involved in the crucifixion of Jesus, namely, 'Herod and Pontius Pilate, with the Gentiles and the peoples of Israel' (Acts 4.27). Once again we have the comment that God or the Holy Spirit speaks through David and the psalm acts as confirmation that the crucifixion was not simply a miscarriage of justice; it was 'whatever your hand and your plan had predestined to take place' (Acts 4.28). In the process, it is asserted that the 'anointed one' (Greek – *christos*) of the psalm is 'your holy servant Jesus, whom you anointed' (Acts 4.27). In the Gospel, Luke has Jesus cite words from Isaiah 61.1 to the effect that he has been 'anointed' to preach 'good news to the poor' (Luke 4.18). If Luke has a particular incident in mind, it is probably Jesus' baptism, where the Holy Spirit descended upon him (Luke 3.22). Thus we have further support from the Psalms that David spoke about Messiah Jesus.

Servant

In the above example, not only is it stated that Jesus is the anointed one (or Messiah) of Psalm 2, he is also referred to as 'your holy servant'. The phrase is repeated in verse 30, where signs and wonders are said to be 'performed through the name of your holy servant Jesus'. Some have argued that this should be taken as an allusion to the suffering servant of Isaiah 53 but it should be noted that in the introduction to the psalm quotation, David is also referred to as God's servant ('Sovereign Lord ... it is you who said by the Holy Spirit through our ancestor David, your servant'). Certainly the reference to 'holy servant' sets Jesus apart from other 'servants' but it does not bring us closer to Isaiah 53. The word 'holy' is used over 60 times in Isaiah but never of the servant and never in Isaiah 53. On its own, it is hard to see how this passage would suggest a reference to Isaiah's suffering servant.

However, there are two other passages that might make the allusion more convincing. The first occurs in Peter's second speech in Acts 3, which begins: 'The God of Abraham, the God of Isaac, and the God of Jacob, the God of our ancestors has glorified his servant Jesus' (Acts 3.13). Once again, it is not clear that calling Jesus 'servant' here is supposed to set him apart from the other named figures – especially as all three are referred to as God's servants somewhere in Scripture (Ps. 105.6; Dan. 4.35;[13] Isa. 44.1). But it is the use of the word 'glorified' (*doxazō*) that has convinced many that this is an allusion to the LXX of Isaiah 52.13, which says: 'Behold, my servant will

21

understand and he will be exalted and glorified (*doxazō*) greatly'.[14] When it is remembered that in Peter's first speech, Jesus is said to have been 'exalted' (Acts 2.33), and that Isaiah 52.13 LXX is the only text in Scripture to speak of a servant being 'glorified', it seems likely that this text is in mind. This is further strengthened by the observation that the speech that ensues appears to follow the main contours of Isaiah 53. As Peter Mallen says:

> The Isaiah 53 passage goes on to explain the rejection of the servant by his audience; his suffering, death and burial as a transgressor; his innocence; and his vindication by God. The Acts 3 passage contains similar elements as Jesus is rejected by the people (3.13–14); suffers (3.18); is killed (3.15a); and then vindicated by being raised from the dead (3.15b, 26) and glorified (3.13). Hence the pattern of Jesus' suffering followed by exaltation is similar to that of the servant.[15]

The other passage has already been considered, namely, the explicit quotation of Isaiah 53.7–8 in Acts 8.32–33. Although we are not told what use Philip made of the passage, there is no doubt about where it comes from. Thus it could be argued that while the use of the word 'servant' in Acts 3.13, 26 and 4.25, 27 is not conclusive, when the reader reaches the explicit quotation in Acts 8, it will confirm that Luke has had Isaiah's servant in mind all along.

A different suggestion is put forward by Peter Doble. It is clear from what we have studied so far that Luke's primary source for understanding Jesus is the Psalms. More than that, it is the figure of David himself, who is named 12 times in Acts, which attracts Luke's interest. And David is specifically called God's servant in Acts 4.25, just before Jesus is referred to as God's 'holy servant'. There is no exact parallel for 'holy servant' in Scripture but in one of the passages where David is called servant, it is said that God anointed him with 'holy oil' (Ps. 89.20). Thus the main titles of Lord, Messiah and servant are all closely linked with David. Doble acknowledges that Acts 3.13 may contain an allusion to Isaiah 52.13 but argues that the principal background for 'servant' in Luke–Acts is David.[16]

Son of God

There are only two references to Jesus as God's son in Acts. The first comes in Luke's summary of what Paul used to proclaim about Jesus in the synagogues: 'He is the Son of God' (Acts 9.20). Nothing further is said but in his speech at Pisidian Antioch, he supports the statement with a quotation from Psalm 2:

> And we bring you the good news that what God promised to our ancestors he has fulfilled for us, their children, by raising Jesus; as also it is written in the second psalm, 'You are my Son; today I have begotten you.'　　　(Acts 13.32–33)

At first glance, this looks as if it is being offered as support for Jesus' resurrection, but the following verse appears to take up this theme for the first time: '*As to* his raising him from the dead, no more to return to corruption', which is then supported by the two texts already discussed (Isa. 55.3; Ps. 16.10). Many scholars, therefore, take the phrase 'raising Jesus' in this verse in the more general sense of 'bringing him on the stage of history'[17] (as in Luke 1.69; Acts 3.22). Thus the 'today I have begotten you' is not a reference to the resurrection and is probably not a reference to his birth either, though it might be included. It is most likely a reference to his baptism, partly because this is when Jesus' public ministry began and partly because the words at the baptism ('You are my Son, the Beloved; with you I am well pleased' – Luke 3.22) contain an echo of Psalm 2. The psalm refers to the appointment or perhaps renewal of David's kingship by God. It is applied to Jesus in a heightened sense of 'Messianic king' but does not seem to have undergone the metaphysical reflection that will lead to John 1.1–18, where 'son' indicates divinity. It also offers further support for Doble's thesis that David is Luke's prime model for understanding Jesus.

Prophet like Moses

The quotation from Deuteronomy 18 in Peter's second speech is somewhat surprising. He has already spoken of Jesus as 'servant' (Acts 3.13), 'Holy and Righteous One' (Acts 3.14), 'Author of life' (Acts 3.15) and 'Messiah' (Acts 3.18). He then seems to digress:

> Moses said, 'The Lord your God will raise up for you from your own people a prophet like me. You must listen to whatever he tells you. And it will be that everyone who does not listen to that prophet will be utterly rooted out from the people.' And all the prophets, as many as have spoken, from Samuel and those after him, also predicted these days. (Acts 3.22–24)

The quotation, which combines phrases from Deuteronomy 18.15–19 with Leviticus 23.29, appears to make two points. The first is that 'listening to Jesus' is the decisive criterion for who belongs to the people of God and who is excluded. This latter point is strengthened by the substitution of Leviticus 23.29 ('utterly rooted out from the people') for the somewhat weaker phrase in Deuteronomy 18.19 ('I myself will hold accountable'). The second point is that Moses, like all the prophets from Samuel onwards, predicted (lit. 'proclaimed') these days. The seeming innovation that membership of the people of God will henceforth be determined by one's response to Jesus is thus supported by the statement that Moses and all the prophets spoke about such a day. It almost seems incidental that the implication of citing Deuteronomy 18 is that Jesus is the 'prophet like Moses', though we know from Qumran (4Q175) that the identity of this prophet was a matter of great interest.

There is a further occurrence in Stephen's speech but once again the content is muted. Stephen is building up to an accusation that the wilderness generation rejected Moses and offered sacrifices to an idol (Acts 7.41) and in order to exacerbate the point, he lists the achievements of Moses. He is the one who tried to help an Israelite against an Egyptian attacker (Acts 7.23–29), who saw the burning bush (Acts 7.30–34), who led them out of Egypt (Acts 7.36) and who said, 'God will raise up a prophet for you from your own people as he raised me up' (Acts 7.37). The promise is not applied to Christ, though after reading Acts 3, the reader will no doubt make the connection. But its occurrence here seems to be nothing more than one of the notable things for which Moses is remembered.

Cornerstone

We have already seen how Psalm 118.22 is used to support Jesus' rejection by referring to him as the 'stone that was rejected by you, the builders' (Acts 4.11). However, the psalm goes on to make the positive point that the rejected stone has become the cornerstone (lit. 'head of the corner'). There is debate as to whether the stone is envisaged at the bottom of the building, where it provides the direction for the walls, or at the top, where it completes the building ('capstone'). Either way, the point is that the stone that has been rejected by one group of builders is seen as utterly essential – precious, as 1 Peter 2.6 puts it – to another group. Therefore it not only encapsulates the rejection–vindication theme for Jesus, it also speaks of its/his rejection by one community and acceptance by another.

Judgement

According to Luke, Scripture not only speaks of the rejection and vindication of Jesus, it also speaks of judgement upon those who rejected him. This begins with Judas, who is said to have 'acquired a field with the reward of his wickedness; and falling headlong, he burst open in the middle and all his bowels gushed out' (Acts 1.18; cf. Matt. 27.3–10 for a different view). Peter has stated that what happened to Judas was foretold by David (through the Holy Spirit) and now quotes from Psalm 69.25 to demonstrate it: 'Let his homestead become desolate, and let there be no one to live in it' (Acts 1.20). The verse comes from a section where David asks God to punish his enemies: 'Let their table be a trap for them' (v. 22); 'Let their eyes be darkened' (v. 23); 'Pour out your indignation upon them' (v. 24); 'May their camp be a desolation' (v. 25); 'Add guilt to their guilt' (v. 27); 'Let them be blotted out of the book of the living' (v. 28). The psalm is frequently applied to Christ in the New Testament (John 2.17; 15.25; Rom. 11.9–10; 15.3) and that is probably how verse 25 came to be associated with Judas. In order for it to apply specifically to Judas, it was necessary to change the plural references to singulars, which makes it rather less convincing to us. But it was an acceptable form of exegesis at the time. It was not that the author was trying to disguise the fact that the original was plural, for that could easily be checked. It was a form of exegesis where the interpretation – Judas embodies the enemies of Christ – is indicated by changing the wording of the quotation from plural to singular.[18]

As well as applying Psalm 2.1–2 ('Why did the Gentiles rage . . . ?') to the rejection of Jesus, the disciples draw the implication that it also explains their own fate: 'And now, Lord, look at their threats, and grant to your servants [lit. "slaves"] to speak your word with all boldness' (Acts 4.29). The theme is not elaborated but seems to suggest that just as the opposition to Jesus was according to God's plan, so it is for them. That is why they can rejoice and ask for boldness, knowing that God will continue to work 'signs and wonders . . . through the name of your holy servant Jesus' (Acts 4.30). The phrase alludes back to Peter's first speech where Jesus is described as a 'man attested to you by God with deeds of power, wonders, and signs that God did through him' (Acts 2.22). Although Jesus is no longer physically present with them, his work continues through the disciples.

As Paul brings his speech at Pisidian Antioch to a close, he issues a warning:

'Beware, therefore, that what the prophets said does not happen to you: "Look, you scoffers! Be amazed and perish, for in your days I am doing a work, a work that you will never believe, even if someone tells you."'   (Acts 13.40–41)

The implication is that those who reject Paul's message are equivalent to the 'scoffers' in the quotation (Hab. 1.5), and will be 'amazed and perish'. This is a strange combination since the word 'amazed' (*thaumazō*) usually has a positive meaning, as when the crowds are 'amazed' at the disciples speaking in other languages (Acts 2.7) or observe the lame man dancing with joy (Acts 3.12). Perhaps we are to understand that unless such 'amazement' results in acceptance and belief, it will lead to destruction.

There is some debate as to whether the introduction ('what the prophets said') is a general reference to what prophets typically say or is an invitation to draw on the particular context of Habakkuk 1.5. If we attempt the latter, we will see that the Hebrew text does not speak of 'scoffers' or 'perish' but says: 'Look at the *nations*, and see! Be astonished! Be *astounded*! For a work is being done in your days that you would not believe if you were told.' However, a commentary on Habakkuk was discovered among the Dead Sea Scrolls and it reads 'traitors' instead of 'nations', so it is possible that the LXX used by Luke was drawing on a Hebrew text like this rather than the one that has come down to us.[19]

If we look at the context of Habakkuk 1.5 for further clarity, it is not very promising. The people will be 'astonished' and 'astounded' because God is going to execute his judgement on the nations by rousing an utterly ruthless nation called the Chaldeans (Babylonians). It is the seeming injustice of this that causes Habakkuk to issue his complaint. But Paul is referring to the surprising way that God will judge 'scoffers' by means of the proclamation of the gospel. Any parallel with Habakkuk's situation is only at a very general level – God sometimes executes his judgement in surprising ways. All in all, it is probably better to see the introduction ('what the prophets said') as a general reference and not an invitation to Theophilus to search for a Habakkuk scroll to discover Luke's meaning.[20]

The book of Acts closes with Paul under house arrest in Rome but with the freedom to entertain fellow Jews and speak to them about Christ (Acts 28.17–22). On one such occasion, the mixed response to his message prompts Paul to quote from Isaiah's commission to preach to a people whose hearts are dull, eyes are shut and ears are hard of hearing. Thus Luke's account of the mission of the Church begins and ends with an extended quotation from the prophets, both of which finish on the need to preach/listen (see Table 1.1).

Table 1.1

Acts 2.17–21/Joel 2.28–32	*Acts 28.25–28/Isaiah 6.9–10*
'In the last days it will be, God declares, that I will pour out my Spirit upon all flesh, and your sons and your daughters shall prophesy, and your young men shall see visions, and your old men shall dream dreams. Even upon my slaves, both men and women, in those days I will pour out my Spirit; and they shall prophesy. And I will show portents in the heaven above and signs on the earth below, blood, and fire, and smoky mist. The sun shall be turned to darkness and the moon to blood, before the coming of the Lord's great and glorious day. *Then everyone who calls on the name of the Lord shall be saved.*'	'The Holy Spirit was right in saying to your ancestors through the prophet Isaiah, "Go to this people and say, You will indeed listen, but never understand, and you will indeed look, but never perceive. For this people's heart has grown dull, and their ears are hard of hearing, and they have shut their eyes; so that they might not look with their eyes, and listen with their ears, and understand with their heart and turn – and I would heal them." *Let it be known to you then that this salvation of God has been sent to the Gentiles; they will listen.*'

Joel's prophecy is mainly positive – a time when God will pour out his spirit on all flesh and 'everyone who calls on the name of the Lord shall be saved'. However, connotations of judgement are present in the symbolism (blood, fire, smoke) and cosmic disturbances (sun darkened, moon turned to blood). Judgement is also present in Joel's concept of the coming 'Day of the Lord', although this is somewhat lost in translation. The Hebrew of Joel 2.31 speaks of the 'great and terrible day' (NIV 'dreadful') but the LXX has rendered the second word with *epiphanē*, assuming the root to be from the word 'see' rather than the word 'fear'. Even so, *epiphanēs* means something like 'manifest' or 'notable', whereas 'glorious' sounds explicitly positive. Thus according to Barrett, Joel's '*great day* of the Lord is the last day, of salvation for his people and destruction for his enemies'.[21]

As we have progressed through Luke's story, we have seen a mixed response from both Jews and Gentiles but as the narrative draws to a close, judgement is focused on the Jews. Despite stating that some Jews were convinced by Paul's preaching (Acts 28.24), Paul appears to lose patience and declares that the message of salvation has been sent to the Gentiles and they will listen. This is no doubt good news for Theophilus, but how does the quotation support his conclusion? By saying that it was addressed to 'your ancestors', he is drawing on a 'like father, like son' argument. So, just as Isaiah preached to a people who were unable to respond because they had closed their eyes once too often ('grown dull'), it is the same for Paul. However, there is nothing in the quotation that suggests a more favourable outcome for Gentiles and perhaps Theophilus is meant to recall the speech at Pisidian Antioch where Isaiah 49.6 is quoted: 'I have set you to be a light for the Gentiles, so that you may bring salvation to the ends of the earth' (Acts 13.47).

A further point of debate is whether Luke regards the rejection of the Jews as final. We know from Romans 9—11 that this was not Paul's view. He believed that the unbelief of the

Jews was temporary and that once the full number of the Gentiles had been brought in, Israel would be grafted back again (Rom. 11.23–26). Luke shows no knowledge of this but there is no reason to assume that the statement that the salvation of God has been sent to the Gentiles implies that it is no longer offered to the Jews. The book of Acts ends with Paul spending two years in Rome and welcoming *all* who came to him (Acts 28.30). There is no reason to assume that this does not include fellow Jews.

Historical summary

Two of the speeches (Stephen and Paul) begin by recounting certain aspects of Israel's history (cf. Pss. 78, 106; Ezek. 20). Stephen's is the fullest, mentioning the following characters: Abraham and the promise of land; Joseph and the famine of Egypt; Moses and the exodus, burning bush and golden calf; David, who desired to build a house for God; and Solomon who built the temple. Paul's speech is more general, speaking of the growth of the people in Egypt, their rebellion in the wilderness, the period of judges up until Samuel, Israel's first king, the disappointing Saul, followed by David, the man after God's heart. As well as the historical references, Stephen's speech also contains the promise of a prophet like Moses (Acts 7.37), a quotation from Amos 5.25–27 to underline Israel's rebellion in the wilderness (Acts 7.42–43), and a quotation of Isaiah 66.1–2 that 'the Most High does not dwell in houses made by human hands' (Acts 7.48). As we have seen, Paul's speech contains quotations from Psalm 2.7 ('You are my Son'), Isaiah 55.3 ('I will give you [plural] the holy promises'), Psalm 16.10 ('You will not let your Holy One experience corruption') and Habakkuk 1.5 ('Look, you scoffers!').

What is the purpose of these historical summaries? In Paul's speech, the emphasis is on fulfilment, both in its positive aspect – Jesus is the Saviour promised to David – and in its negative aspect – those who condemned him were unwittingly fulfilling Scripture. We are not told which Scriptures are in mind but they presumably include those already quoted in Acts, namely, the rejected stone of Psalm 118, the sheep led to slaughter in Isaiah 53 and perhaps God's anointed in Psalm 2. For Luke, the 'residents of Jerusalem and their leaders' have no excuse for not recognizing Jesus for the 'prophets . . . are read every sabbath' (Acts 13.27).

As to the positive statement that Jesus is the Saviour promised to David, one searches in vain for such a text. The Greek term *sōtēr* is applied to God around 20 times in the Old Testament and on two occasions, it is said that 'besides me there is no saviour' (Isa. 43.11; Hos. 13.4). Presumably Luke is thinking more generally of promises of redemption/salvation and possibly associating it with David through a text like Psalm 132, which was alluded to in Acts 2.30:

> The LORD swore to David a sure oath from which he will
>   not turn back:
> 'One of the sons of your body I will set on your throne . . .
> For the LORD has chosen Zion; he has desired it for his
>   habitation . . .
> Its priests I will clothe with salvation, and its faithful will
>   shout for joy.
> There I will cause a horn to sprout up for David; I have
>   prepared a lamp for my anointed one . . . '
>   (Psalm 132.11, 13, 16, 17)

Stephen's speech is rather different. After recounting the history of the patriarchs, he focuses on how Israel rejected Moses, the one whom God had raised up to lead them out of Egypt. He does this first by reciting the incident where Moses came to the aid of a fellow Israelite and was rebuffed with the words, 'Who made you a ruler and a judge over us?' (Acts 7.27/Exod. 2.14). This is repeated in Acts 7.35, though it is difficult to see why Luke gives it such prominence. He then describes the rebellion in the wilderness and the idolatry of the golden calf ('Our ancestors were unwilling to obey him; instead, they pushed him aside, and in their hearts they turned back to Egypt' – Acts 7.39). What they did not realize was that their rebellion against Moses was rebellion against God, as confirmed by a quotation from Amos 5.25–27. We then have a section on God's dwelling place (Acts 7.44–50) before the author indicts his hearers with the words:

> 'You stiff-necked people, uncircumcised in heart and ears, you are for ever opposing the Holy Spirit, just as your ancestors used to do. Which of the prophets did your ancestors not persecute? They killed those who foretold the coming of the Righteous One, and now you have become his betrayers and murderers.'
>
> (Acts 7.51–52)

Thus the history is primarily recounted in order to show that Israel has always resisted God's plan to save and that is precisely the case now. What is difficult to understand, however, is the role of Acts 7.44–50. We are first told of the 'tent of testimony' that God commanded Moses to build. This remained in existence 'until the time of David, who found favour with God and asked that he might find a dwelling-place for the house of Jacob' (Acts 7.45–46). Such a house was built by Solomon but Stephen then quotes Isaiah 66.1–2 that God 'does not dwell in houses made by human hands' (Acts 7.48). Are we to understand that the building of the temple is another illustration of Israel's rebellion? And if so, are David and Solomon both guilty or does verse 47 ('*But* it was Solomon') lay all the blame at Solomon's feet?

Barrett notes that the adversatives of verse 47 ('*But* it was Solomon') and verse 48 ('*Yet* the Most High') can be taken in either a weak sense ('Solomon built a house for God, but we must not think that God is confined to it') or a strong sense ('Solomon built a house for God, but this was a complete misunderstanding of the nature of God and should not have been done').[22] F. F. Bruce prefers the former, arguing that Solomon was well aware that the heavens cannot contain God, let alone his temple (1 Kings 8.27). Solomon's 'mistake' was essentially a christological one: the son of David who will build a house for God was in fact a reference to Christ. Thus what is being deprecated is not the temple itself – which the apostles continue to attend (Acts 1—5) – but the 'state of mind to which the temple gave rise – a state of mind which the mobile tabernacle could not have engendered'.[23]

Barrett agrees with Bruce's christological understanding but draws a different conclusion: 'In providing an abode for God Solomon wrongfully anticipated the work of Christ; the *oikos* [house] he provided was in contravention of the prophetic principle stated in v. 48.'[24] Such a view is in keeping with Stephen's use of Amos 5.25–27 to denounce the whole wilderness period as a time of idolatry (Acts 7.42–43) and the exaggeration that is included in Stephen's indictment ('Which of the prophets did your ancestors not persecute?'). Barrett acknowledges that in the context of Isaiah 66, the critique of verses 1–2 does not amount to a total repudiation of the temple, but he thinks this is how Stephen (Luke) chose to read it. Stephen is not just denouncing a 'misunderstanding' of the temple but the temple itself.

On the other hand, other scholars have argued that more weight should be given to the context of Isaiah 66.1–2. There is clearly a strong denunciation of sacrifice ('Whoever slaughters an ox is like one who kills a human being' – Isa. 66.3a), but this is in contrast to 'the humble and contrite in spirit, who trembles at my word' (Isa. 66.2b). Mallen argues that Stephen is in agreement with this but his application is diametrically opposite to that of his accusers. They think that they are the 'humble and contrite' while Stephen and his associates are those who delight in their abominations (Isa. 66.3b). Stephen reverses this, claiming that it is they who are guilty of killing the righteous one and thus correspond to all those rebellious Israelites who previously opposed God's plan of salvation:

For readers who know the context in Isaiah, Luke has presented a severe prophetic critique of Stephen's opponents and reversed the charges: they face God's rejection and judgement, exemplified in the later destruction of the Jerusalem Temple (Lk. 13.35; 19.43–44; 21.20–24; 23.27–31).[25]

Major interpretations of Acts and Scripture

The majority of scholars believe that Acts is the sequel to the Gospel of Luke and so any account of 'Acts and Scripture' must also do justice to what we find in the Gospel. In particular, it has been argued that the opening quotations and allusions of Luke's Gospel provide the reader with an interpretative framework to understand the rest of the narrative ('Luke–Acts'). The major question has been whether that should be the Isaiah quotations that surround the beginning of Jesus' ministry in Luke 3—4 or the allusions that are embedded in the various promises of Luke 1—2. The former leads to the view that Isaiah is Luke's most important influence, with major quotations occurring at key points in the Gospel (Luke 3.4–6; 4.18–19; 8.10; 19.46; 22.37) and continuing in Acts (Acts 7.49–50; 8.32–33; 13.34; 13.47; 28.26–27). The latter leads to various views, including the theory of Peter Doble, that Luke's Christology is modelled on David and the Psalms. Kenneth Litwak interprets the evidence differently, believing that the multiple references show that Luke is not intending to highlight a specific text or theme but to show that *all* the events narrated in the double work are in continuity with Scripture. This is why specific texts are not mentioned in the summaries.[26] We will begin with Doble's theory.

Acts and the songs of David

There are four main arguments in support of Doble's theory. The first is the simple fact that there are far more explicit quotations from the Psalms (11) in Acts than there are from Isaiah

(5). When Luke wants to show that Jesus' resurrection and exaltation is supported by Scripture, he turns to Psalms 16 and 110. When he wants support for the rejection and persecution of Jesus, he turns to Psalms 2 and 118. And when he wants support for the sonship of Jesus, it is the words addressed to David in Psalm 2.7 that he quotes. Any theory about how Luke uses Scripture in Luke–Acts must account for this focus on the Psalms in the early Acts speeches.

Second, he notes that most of these psalms are also prominent in Luke's Gospel and anticipate the clarifications offered in Acts. Thus Psalm 2.7 ('You are my Son') is alluded to at Jesus' baptism (Luke 3.16) and transfiguration (Luke 9.35) but explicitly applied to Jesus in Paul's speech, where its source is specifically mentioned ('as also it is written in the second psalm' – Acts 13.33).[27] Psalm 110 ('The Lord said to my Lord') is quoted by Jesus in Luke 20.42–43 but is left as a puzzle ('David thus calls him Lord; so how can he be his son?'). It is clarified when Peter applies it to Jesus in his Pentecost speech, for 'David's son can also be David's "lord" because God raised him from the dead, gave him David's throne for ever, and made him Lord and Christ'.[28] And Psalm 118 ('The stone that the builders rejected') is quoted at the end of the parable of the vineyard (Luke 20.17), implying that the son who is killed in the parable is the rejected stone. This is made explicit in Acts 4.11. The exception is Psalm 16, which does not appear in Luke's Gospel or indeed in any other New Testament writing.

Third, before we get to the Isaiah quotations in Luke 3—4, Gabriel announces to Mary that God will give Jesus 'the throne of his ancestor David' (Luke 1.32) and Zechariah says that God has 'raised up a mighty saviour for us in the house of his servant David' (Luke 1.69). David is mentioned 24 times in Luke–Acts and specifically as the one who speaks through the Psalms on 6 occasions (Luke 20.42; Acts 1.16; 2.25, 31, 34; 4.25). In contrast, Isaiah is only mentioned by name on 5 occasions (Luke 3.4; 4.17; Acts 8.28, 30; 28.25) and although such statistics should be treated with caution, it is surely significant that the reader is constantly hearing the name 'David'.

Fourth, Doble notes how scholars have searched in vain to find a prophetic text that predicts a suffering Messiah and have had to settle for a suffering servant. But God's anointed (*christos*) in the Psalms 'suffered and stood in horror of Hades, from whose confines he trusted God to free him'.[29] Not only does Jesus quote words of David (Psalm 31.5) in the hour of his death (Luke 23.46), it is clear from the Acts speeches that his death and resurrection are understood in the light of the Psalms. Thus Doble suggests that the most likely background for Jesus as God's servant is not Isaiah 53 but David, God's anointed son.

Acts and Isaiah

Others have argued that Isaiah is the most important influence on Luke. Some focus on the suffering servant theme, believing that the explicit quotation in Luke 22.37 ('And he was counted among the lawless' – Isa. 53.12) supports the quotation in Acts 8.32–33 ('Like a sheep he was led to the slaughter') and confirms that Luke's narrative of the rejection, vindication and exaltation of Jesus is based on Isaiah's fourth servant song. Supporting evidence comes from the glorification of the servant in Acts 3.13, which can be uniquely traced to Isaiah 52.13, and Jesus as 'the Righteous One' (Acts 3.14; 7.52; 22.14), which is plausibly linked to Isaiah 53.11. It is clear from texts like John 12.38, Romans 10.16 and 1 Peter 2.21–25 that Isaiah 53 was an important text in the early Church and Luke–Acts offers further support for this. Luke might use Psalm 16 when he wants to argue that the particular *form* of Jesus' vindication/exaltation was resurrection but it is Isaiah's suffering servant that provides the underlying framework for his narrative.

A broader theory is offered by David Pao, who observes that it is not so much Isaiah 53 that is prominent in Luke–Acts but Isaiah 40—55. He notes that Jesus' public ministry is announced with an extended quotation from Isaiah 40.3–5. In Isaiah, this is part of a prologue (Isa. 40.1–11) that introduces the key themes of Isaiah 40—55, namely, release from captivity, proclamation of the word of God, conquest of enemies, giving of the Spirit and God teaching his people. These themes are all connected with the exodus narratives and many scholars have argued that Isaiah views the future deliverance of God as a New Exodus. It is Pao's view that the quotation of Isaiah 40.3–5 at the very beginning of Jesus' ministry plays a similar role for the rest of Luke–Acts. Thus the command to make a 'way' in the desert is fulfilled in the Christian community, which is regularly referred to as 'the Way' (Acts 9.2; 19.9, 23; 22.4; 24.14). The promise that the 'word of our God will stand for ever' (Isa. 40.8) corresponds to the frequent references in Acts to the word of God leading and directing events (Acts 6.7; 12.24; 13.46). And one of the key features of Isaiah 40—55 is that the good news will be preached to Gentiles. This is announced in the quotation of Isaiah 40.5 in Luke 3.6 ('and all flesh shall see the salvation of God'), repeated in Jesus' commission to take the gospel to the Gentiles in Luke 24.47 and Acts 1.8, and confirmed in the quotation of Isaiah 49.6 in Paul's Antioch speech ('I have set you to be a light for the Gentiles, so that you may bring salvation to the ends of the earth' – Acts 13.47). For Pao, the underlying structure of Luke–Acts is the New Exodus as expounded in Isaiah 40—55 and so 'ecclesiological' is a more accurate description of Luke's use of Scripture than 'christological'.[30]

Many scholars find this broadly convincing and it is clear that the major themes of Isaiah 40—55 are present in Acts. However, it should be noted that the relative prominence of the themes in Acts does not necessarily correspond to their prominence in Isaiah. For example, while there are texts like Isaiah 49.6 that envisage Gentiles joining the people of God, the emphasis in Isaiah is overwhelmingly on the restoration and glorification of Israel (and Jerusalem). This is the reverse

of Acts, which ends with Paul indicting the Jews for their blind-
ness (using Isa. 6.9–10, a text outside the framework of chapters 40—55) and suggesting that it is the Gentiles who will
listen (Acts 28.25–29). Pao speaks of this as a reinterpretation
and in some ways he is correct. But it raises doubts as to whether
Isaiah 40—55 can properly be called a 'framework' for interpreting Acts. Luke's reinterpretation comes from the fact (as he
understands it) that the gospel has received far greater acceptance among Gentiles than it has among Jews. That he understands this as the fulfilment of Isaiah 6.9–10 is significant for
the overall importance of Isaiah to Luke but it does not support
Pao's thesis. As Peter Mallen says:

> The New Exodus hope for the restoration of Israel, clearly
> sounded at the beginning of the narrative and partially fulfilled
> in the opening chapters of Acts, threatens to unravel completely
> by the end of the narrative. Gentiles have apparently become
> the predominant part of God's restored people and Luke's
> readers would probably be aware that Jerusalem now lies in
> ruins. One must therefore seriously question the claim that the
> New Exodus provides the hermeneutical key to understand the
> entire narrative.[31]

Mallen thinks these limitations are largely overcome if one
replaces 'New Exodus' by the 'dual mission of the servant'. He
does not understand this in the narrow sense of establishing
doctrines of atonement or Christology from Isaiah 53, which
characterized much of the older debate, but as 'furnishing a
job description or outline for Jesus' mission and that of his
followers'.[32] Although the servant passages do not explicitly say
that the inclusion of the Gentiles will be on an equal basis with
the restoration of Israel, neither do they say the opposite. Mallen
thinks this is a significant difference to the New Exodus theme,
which explicitly prioritizes Israel. He also notes that the oscil-
lation between the individual and corporate characteristics of
Isaiah's servant lends itself to the application of Jesus and his

followers. However, it should be noted that Mallen also uses the literary concept of intertextuality[33] to argue that not only has Isaiah shaped Luke's narrative, the events that he has recorded have shaped his interpretation of Isaiah: 'The selected Isaianic passages help the audience to understand Jesus and his mission, while Jesus in turn helps to interpret the role of the servant and the nature of salvation in Isaiah.'[34] He thus speaks of the 'dual mission of the servant' as better reflecting 'Luke's reading of Isaiah' rather than speaking about 'frameworks' or 'hermeneutical lenses'.

Conclusion

It has been a prominent theme in recent scholarship on 'Acts and Scripture' that narratives can be as important as speeches and allusions as important as quotations. The point is well made but one should also issue a caution: allusions are by definition elusive and there is often debate as to their exact source. It would therefore be unwise to play down the significance of the explicit quotations. For example, if it is true that Luke's Gospel establishes an Isaian framework for understanding Acts, Theophilus would surely be a little perplexed that the speeches in Acts 1—5 revolve around the Psalms rather than Isaiah. Indeed, the first quotation from Isaiah does not appear until well into the story (Acts 7.49–50/Isa. 66.1–2) and its subject is not the servant. Mallen is no doubt correct that Peter's second speech (Acts 3.12–26) contains an allusion to Isaiah 52.13 and possibly some echoes to the rest of the song, but this should not be used to negate the evidence of the quotations. Either Theophilus is being asked to think historically and deduce that Luke's emphasis on Isaiah was not shared by the historical Peter or the emphasis on an Isaian framework has been overdone.

I am inclined to favour the latter and Peter's second speech provides a good example of why. It is clearly possible to pick out a few phrases from the speech (glorified servant, righteous one, rejected, suffer) and show how they can be linked to the vocation of the servant, but we must also take into account those things that point in other directions. For example, rather than inviting the reader to focus on Isaiah, the speech refers to 'all the prophets' (Acts 3.18, 24), 'his holy prophets' (Acts 3.21), 'Moses said' (Acts 3.22) and 'saying to Abraham' (Acts 3.25). The thrust is not to focus on one passage but to show that 'the law of Moses, the prophets, and the psalms' (Luke 24.44) are being fulfilled. And even in verses 13–14, where the servant language is most prominent, there are other phrases that 'scatter' the reader's attention. Thus if Luke had wanted his readers to take 'Righteous one' as a reference to Isaiah 53.11, why make it more difficult by speaking of the 'Holy and Righteous one' and adding 'Author of life' in the next sentence?

More significantly, it has often been pointed out that the major correspondence between the fourth servant song and Jesus is the voluntary nature of his suffering, expressed in the phrase, 'he poured out himself to death' (Isa. 53.12). But this is not the emphasis of Peter's speeches. Peter says of his hearers: '*you* handed over and rejected' (Acts 3.13); '*you* rejected the Holy and Righteous one' (Acts 3.14); '*you* killed the Author of life' (Acts 3.15). It is true that through these actions, God fulfilled what the prophets foretold, but 'voluntary suffering' is not a specific theme in Peter's speeches. Of course, one can turn this around and say that there is no reason why Peter should include every element from Isaiah 53 but my point is not to deny any influence of Isaiah but to deny that it was a *controlling* influence.

A similar point could be made about the possible allusion to Isaiah in Acts 1.8: 'But you will receive power when the Holy Spirit has come upon you; and you will be my witnesses in Jerusalem, in all Judea and Samaria, and to the ends of the earth.' Given the explicit quotation of Isaiah 49.6 in Acts 13.47, it is quite plausible that the phrase 'to the ends of the earth' is an earlier allusion to that verse or others like it in Isaiah (Isa.

45.22; 48.20; 62.11). But it is difficult to see why this should take precedence over the explicit quotation of Joel that begins Peter's Pentecost speech. As well as the immediate application of Joel to the outpouring of the Spirit, it introduces important ecclesial themes that will figure in the rest of Acts: people will indeed see visions, utter prophecies and call on the name of the Lord. The lack of any other quotations or significant allusions to Joel in Acts shows that it is not offering a 'Joel framework' for interpreting Acts but neither was it important for Luke to highlight an Isaiah text at this key point of the narrative.

Thus in terms of the servant imagery in Acts, it seems likely that Luke draws on both Isaiah and the Psalms. Neither one 'controls' his narrative but both have had an important influence on his writings. This has not happened in a vacuum, however, as if Luke studied the Scriptures and then deduced what happened to Jesus and the disciples. He was also influenced by the historical traditions that came down to him (Luke 1.1–4). There is much debate as to the nature of these traditions but if it is correct that Mark was one of his sources for writing the Gospel, then we see an author who is both conservative with his sources and free to change the emphasis when it suits his purposes.[35] It is possible that the themes that we have highlighted in this study simply reflect the themes he found in his sources, but if the parallel with Mark's Gospel holds good, we might hazard a guess that he has accentuated the role of certain psalms (2, 16, 110, 118, 132) and key sections of Isaiah (6, 49, 52—53, 66), along with the promises to Abraham in Genesis 12, 15, 17, 22 and Moses in Deuteronomy 18 (and his role in Exodus 1—3, 32). What holds these passages together is not found in the Old Testament itself but in the Christian traditions concerning Jesus and his followers.

2

1 Peter and Scripture

Introduction

Although the order of the books in the New Testament would suggest that we turn to Hebrews next, it will be more useful to follow Acts with a study of 1 Peter, since the first part of Acts was devoted to Peter's speeches. In particular, it will be interesting to see if 1 Peter makes use of the same psalm texts to speak about Christ's persecution (Ps. 2.1–2), rejection (Ps. 118.22), resurrection (Ps. 16.8–11) and exaltation (Ps. 110.1), along with inheriting the throne of David from Psalm 132.11. There is debate among scholars as to whether the polished Greek of 1 Peter could have come from a fisherman like Peter and some suggest that Silvanus, who is mentioned in 1 Peter 5.12 ('Through Silvanus, whom I consider a faithful brother, I have written this short letter'), might have had a rather greater role in its composition than was usual for secretaries. Indeed, some scholars suggest that it was not written by Peter at all but a later disciple writing in his name.[1] The debate is important but not crucial for our study, since it is also disputed whether the speeches attributed to Peter in Acts are his actual words or what Luke believed Peter would have said on the various occasions. We will see at the end of our study if our results have any bearing on this question.[2]

1 Peter and the Psalms

There are only two quotations from the Psalms in 1 Peter. The first is the rejected stone passage from Psalm 118.22, which now appears between two other 'stone' texts, Isaiah 28.16 ('See,

I am laying in Zion a stone') and Isaiah 8.14 ('A stone that makes them stumble'). In Acts, Peter is addressing the rulers and elders of Jerusalem and argues that they fulfilled the psalm when they crucified Jesus, but the stone that they rejected has become the cornerstone of a new building. The author of 1 Peter is writing to the dispersed Christians of Asia (1 Pet. 1.1) and makes the point that to those who believe, Jesus is precious, but 'for those who do not believe, "The stone that the builders rejected has become the very head of the corner"' (1 Pet. 2.7). Clearly he cannot accuse them directly of crucifying Jesus, as in Acts, but the psalm is being used in a similar way: what is rejected by one group of people is fundamental to the lives of another group.

The second quotation comes in the middle of the letter and is from Psalm 34.12–16. The familiar dictum that one should not 'repay evil for evil' (Matt. 5.44; Rom. 12.17; 1 Thess. 5.15) is quoted in 1 Peter 3.9 and then supported by the words of the psalm:

> Those who desire life and desire to see good days, let them keep their tongues from evil and their lips from speaking deceit; let them turn away from evil and do good; let them seek peace and pursue it. For the eyes of the Lord are on the righteous, and his ears are open to their prayer. But the face of the Lord is against those who do evil.　　　　　　　　(1 Peter 3.10–12)

As with Psalm 118.22, the quoted words envisage two groups of people. In this case, the contrast is between those who 'seek peace' and those who use their 'tongues' and 'lips' to do evil, suggesting that the author has malicious speech in mind. He has already quoted the example of Christ ('When he was abused, he did not return abuse' – 1 Pet. 2.23) and will draw the conclusion that any defence of the faith must be done with 'gentleness and reverence' (1 Pet. 3.16). As in the Acts speeches, it might be the ascription to David that led to the psalm but its use here is ethical rather than christological. It is not quoted elsewhere in the New Testament and appears to be the author's own discovery. It is clearly important to him, for not only is it the longest quotation in the letter, there is also an allusion to verse 8 of the psalm in 1 Peter 2.3. The striking imagery that the readers have 'tasted that the Lord is good' comes from Psalm 34.8, which begins with an invitation: 'O taste and see that the Lord is good'. Eugene Boring suggests that this might have been facilitated by the fact that the Greek word for 'good' is *chrēstos*, which would have been pronounced much the same as *christos* in the first century.[3] Karen Jobes goes further. She thinks that the themes of the psalm, namely, deliverance from shame (34.5), affliction (34.6) and want (34.9–10), are precisely what the readers of 1 Peter are facing:

> His logic appears to be that just as God delivered David from his sojourn among the Philistines, God will deliver the Asian Christians from the afflictions caused by their faith in Christ, because they are no less God's covenant people than was David.[4]

These two examples show that the Psalms were important to the author but in comparison to the Acts speeches, there is a significant difference: they are not used to explain the suffering, death and resurrection of Christ. He does of course use the same 'rejected stone' passage from Psalm 118.22 but it is the two Isaiah passages that largely control the meaning; he does not dwell on the psalm's significance for understanding Jesus. As for the other quotation, it is clear from its length, pivotal position and similarity of context that Psalm 34 is important to him but its use is primarily ethical. We should also mention the allusions in 1 Peter 3.22, where the author asserts that Jesus has 'gone into heaven and is *at the right hand of God*, with angels, authorities, and powers *made subject to him*'. The italicized phrases go back to Psalm 110.1 and Psalm 8.7 respectively, but unlike 1 Corinthians 15.24–28 and Hebrews 1.13—2.9, they are not subject to exposition or reflection. They are simply part of an inherited tradition that the author assumes is common to him and his readers.

1 Peter and Isaiah

As we saw in Chapter 1, there is some doubt as to whether Isaiah is a significant feature of Peter's speeches in Acts. There is no such doubt in 1 Peter, with six explicit quotations (Isa. 8.14; 28.16; 40.6–8; 43.20; 43.21; 53.9) and a number of significant allusions (Isa. 8.13; 11.1; 53.4, 5, 6, 7, 12). The first quotation comes from the important 'voice in the wilderness' chapter (Isaiah 40), which is quoted in the Gospels and Paul. However, the verses quoted in 1 Peter are not v. 3 (Matt. 3.3; Mark 1.3; Luke 3.4; John 1.17), vv. 4–5 (Luke 3.5–6) or v. 13 (Rom. 11.34; 1 Cor. 2.16) but vv. 6–8, where a contrast is made between the transitory nature of human existence and the abiding character of God's word (see Table 2.1).

On the surface, the author's point seems straightforward. He associates the new birth of his readers with imperishable seed,

Table 2.1

Isaiah 40.6–8	*1 Peter 1.23–25*
A voice says, 'Cry out!' And I said, 'What shall I cry?'	You have been born anew, not of perishable but of imperishable seed, through the living and enduring word of God. For
All people are grass, their constancy is like the flower of the field. The grass withers, the flower fades, when the breath of the LORD blows upon it; surely the people are grass.	'All *flesh* is like grass and all its *glory* like the *flower of grass.*
The grass withers, the flower fades; but the word of our God will stand for ever.	The grass withers, and the flower *falls*, but the word of the *Lord* endures for ever.' That word is the good news that was announced to you.

through the agency of the living and enduring word of God. This is then identified as the good news that was preached to them. The quotation confirms the point that God's word is enduring, adding the encouraging 'for ever', while evoking a common experience of things perishable ('grass') and equating this with the lot of 'the flesh'. Jobes also notes the contextual similarity between the two writings: both are addressed to exiles facing persecution and are tempted to doubt the veracity of God's promises. In both cases, the author's response is that the 'word of God' can be trusted because it abides for ever.[5]

The words of Isaiah have been abbreviated somewhat and the differences (*flesh, glory, flower of grass, falls*) are because the author is following the LXX. However, he does make one change from the LXX, substituting 'word of the Lord' for 'word of God'. John Elliott thinks this is deliberate, noting that the author generally uses 'Lord' (*kyrios*) for Jesus (1 Pet. 1.3; 2.2; 3.15) and 'God' (*theos*) for God the Father (1 Pet. 1.2, 3, 5, 21, 23, etc.). Now in such genitive phrases, 'Lord' can be taken as the subject ('the Lord's word') or the object ('the word concerning the Lord'). Elliott thinks it is the latter and so suggests that the author has changed the meaning of the Isaiah passage from 'God's word abides for ever' to 'the word *about* Christ abides for ever'.[6] Ramsey Michaels makes a case for the subjective genitive (Jesus' preaching) but in the end says: 'To Peter, the message of Jesus and the message about Jesus are the same message, just as they are to Mark (1:1, 14–15) and to the author of Hebrews (2:3–4).'[7]

The next Isaiah quotation combines the two stone references in Isaiah 8.14/28.16 with the rejected stone of Psalm 118.22. It has been the focus of much discussion because Paul also combines the two Isaiah texts in Romans 9.33 and shares some of the same differences from the LXX. Thus they both use the verb *tithēmi* instead of the LXX's *embalō* for the first phrase ('I am laying'), omit the reference to 'foundation' and use *skandalon* rather than *ptōmati* for the 'rock of offence/falling' in Isaiah 8.14 (see italics in Table 2.2). It is also of note that in Luke's version of the parable of the vineyard, the quotation of Psalm 118.22 is followed by an allusion to Daniel 2.34 ('Everyone

Table 2.2

Old Testament	1 Peter 2.6–8	Romans 9.33
See, I am laying (*embalō*) in Zion a *foundation stone*, a tested stone, a precious cornerstone, a sure foundation:	'See, I am laying (*tithēmi*) in Zion a stone, a cornerstone chosen and precious;	'See, I am laying (*tithēmi*) in Zion a stone that will make people stumble, a rock that will make them fall (*skandalou*),
'One who trusts will not panic.' (Isa. 28.16)	and whoever believes in him will not be put to shame.'	and whoever believes in him will not be put to shame.'
	To you then who believe, he is precious; but for those who do not believe,	
The stone that the builders rejected has become the chief cornerstone. (Ps. 118.22)	'The stone that the builders rejected has become the very head of the corner', and	
He will become a sanctuary, a stone one strikes against; for both houses of Israel he will become a rock one stumbles over (*ptōmati*) – a trap and a snare for the inhabitants of Jerusalem. (Isa. 8.14)	'A stone that makes them stumble, and a rock that makes them fall (*skandalou*).'	

who falls on that stone will be broken to pieces; and it will crush anyone on whom it falls' – Luke 20.18). It would seem that the early Church went in search of 'stone' texts to deepen their understanding of Christ and it is possible that 1 Peter is drawing on such a collection rather than compiling the texts for himself.[8]

There are two features of the LXX that have facilitated this application of Isaiah 28.16/8.14 to Christ and his followers. In Isaiah 28.16, the phrase, 'one who trusts will not panic', has received a direct object in the LXX. This clarifies that it is the one who trusts *in the stone* that will not panic, or as the LXX has it, 'will not be put to shame'. This may indicate that the LXX is already thinking of the stone as a messianic figure and indeed the pronoun could also be rendered 'him', as it undoubtedly is in 1 Peter and Romans.

Second, the Hebrew of Isaiah 8.14 is confusing in that God is both a 'sanctuary' and 'a stone one strikes against'. The LXX turns this into a contrast: For the one who trusts, God will be a sanctuary and *not* a stone that causes stumbling. First Peter appears to draw on this by saying that the promise of Isaiah 28.16 is applicable to those who believe but for those who do not believe, they face the threat of Isaiah 8.14. The insertion of Psalm 118.22 is curious, since it makes the positive point that the rejected stone has become the 'head of the corner' and so applies to believers rather than unbelievers. Perhaps the point is that as well as stumbling over the stone, unbelievers have to recognize that they are no longer part of the building. As Schutter says, the emphasis is not so much on identifying Christ as the stone but 'primarily to evoke the builders' shame over their mistake and only secondarily to refer to Christ's exaltation.'[9]

The explicit quotations are anticipated in 1 Peter 2.4 by purposely echoing their language: 'Come to him, a living *stone*, though *rejected* by mortals yet *chosen and precious* in God's sight.' This plays an important literary role for had the full text of Isaiah 28.16 been quoted at the beginning, he could not have made the comparison, 'like living stones, let yourselves be built into a spiritual house', for a building is not composed of numerous cornerstones. Schutter calls this a 'midrashic exegesis' of Isaiah 28.16, though others find such a term unhelpful: it suggests that Isaiah 28.16 was a problem to be solved rather than a means to an end.

In the verses that follow (1 Pet. 2.9–10), a series of epithets are applied to the Church which draw on a range of Scriptures. Exodus 19.6 has supplied the phrases 'royal priesthood' and 'holy nation'. The idea that those who were not God's people and had not been shown mercy have become God's people and have been shown mercy comes from Hosea 2.23, which is also quoted by Paul in Romans 9.25. And the idea of a 'chosen race', who were prepared by God to proclaim his mighty acts, comes from Isaiah 43.20–21:

> The wild animals will honour me, the jackals and the ostriches; for I give water in the wilderness, rivers in the desert, to give drink to my *chosen people*, the people whom *I formed for myself so that they might declare my praise*.

The author appears untroubled by the fact that these epithets were originally addressed to Israel and simply assumes that they now apply to the Church. This could be taken as evidence that the author was not the historical Peter, whose mission, according to Galatians 2.7, was to the Jews. Surely he would at least offer some reasoning for how these texts can now be applied to Christians? But it has to be said that the hypothesis that someone is writing in Peter's name faces the same difficulty, for they would not want to present a picture of Peter that was contrary to tradition. The phrase 'who called you out of darkness into his marvellous light' could be a general reference but, in the light of all the other allusions, is perhaps a reference to Isaiah 9.2 ('The people who walked in darkness have seen a great light'), a text quoted in Matthew 4.16.

But you are a *chosen* race, a royal priesthood, a holy nation, God's own *people, in order that you may proclaim the mighty acts of him*[10] who called you out of darkness into his marvellous light. Once you were not a people, but now you are God's people; once you had not received mercy, but now you have received mercy. (1 Peter 2.9–10)

There is considerable doubt as to whether Peter alludes to Isaiah 53 in the Acts speeches but 1 Peter 2.22–25 consists almost entirely of phrases drawn from Isaiah 53.4, 5, 6, 7, 9 and 12 (see Table 2.3). Schutter thinks a pattern can be perceived, with the first half of the passage drawing on the second half of Isaiah 53.4–12 and the second half drawing on the first part. The splice, as he calls it, comes in 1 Peter 2.24, which combines the 'our sins' of Isaiah 53.4 with the 'bore the sin of many' of Isaiah 53.12.

Table 2.3

Isaiah 53.4, 5, 6, 7, 9, 12	*1 Peter 2.22–25*
(A) Surely he has borne our infirmities . . .	(E) 'He committed no sin, and no deceit was found in his mouth.'
(B) upon him was the punishment that made us whole, and by his bruises we are healed.	(D) When he was abused, he did not return abuse; when he suffered, he did not threaten;
(C) All we like sheep have gone astray . . .	(F) but he entrusted himself (*paredidou*) to the one who judges justly.
(D) He was oppressed, and he was afflicted, yet he did not open his mouth . . .	(A, G) He himself bore our sins in his body on the cross, so that, free from sins, we might live for righteousness;
(E) he had done no violence, and there was no deceit in his mouth . . .	(B) by his wounds you have been healed.
(F) he poured out (*paredothē*) himself to death . . .	(C) For you were going astray like sheep, but now you have returned to the shepherd and guardian of your souls.
(G) he bore the sin of many.	

In the context of an exhortation to slaves (1 Pet. 2.18), 1 Peter finds a number of important themes in Isaiah 53. First, although Christ's suffering was unjust ('He committed no sin, and no deceit was found in his mouth'), he did not retaliate or utter abuse. Isaiah says that the servant was 'oppressed, and he was afflicted' but 'there was no deceit in his mouth'. Second, both Isaiah and 1 Peter use the metaphor of 'straying sheep' to describe the situation of the readers. 1 Peter adds, 'but now you have returned to the shepherd and guardian of your souls'. This is probably drawn from Christian tradition, although it might have been suggested by the link between 'turning' and 'healing' found in another Isaiah text (Isa. 6.10[11]) or the 'going astray' and 'returning' of the sheep in Ezekiel 34.4 and 16.[12] Third, Jesus' suffering was not simply the product of injustice and abuse but accomplished something for others: 'He himself bore our sins in his body on the cross . . . by his wounds you have been healed.' Here we have a vicarious role ascribed to Jesus' death that is never made explicit in Acts.

Having quoted the 'stone' saying of Isaiah 8.14, it is interesting that he draws on the preceding verses in 1 Peter 3.14–15. Isaiah warns his hearers not to fear what their opponents fear; rather, they should set apart or sanctify the Lord. Peter has the same contrast between inappropriate fear and sanctifying the Lord but his meaning is somewhat different to that of Isaiah, as Carson explains:

> In Isa. 8:12b, the 'fear' that Isaiah and his followers are not to share is the fear that held their opponents captive, the fear of being taken over by foreign forces from the northeast, prompting the leaders to make an unwise coalition with Egypt. In 1 Pet. 3:14, however, the fear in which Peter's readers are not to indulge is not the fear that their opponents feared but rather the opponents themselves.[13]

The transition is understandable since the particular fears of the opponents would be of no consequence to Peter's readers;

Table 2.4

Isaiah 11.2	1 Peter 4.14
The *spirit of* the LORD shall *rest on* him, the spirit of wisdom and understanding, the spirit of counsel and might, the spirit of knowledge and the fear of the LORD.	If you are reviled for the name of Christ, you are blessed, because the *spirit of* glory, which is the *Spirit of* God, is *resting on* you.

it is the threat that the opponents pose which calls for faith and courage. It should also be noted that once again, the identification of a *kyrios* ('Lord') in Scripture with Christ receives no explanation, although the resulting phrase (lit. 'but sanctify the Lord Christ in your hearts') is somewhat difficult.[14]

Lastly, most scholars find a significant Isaiah allusion in 1 Peter 4.14 (see Table 2.4). The verbal parallels are not extensive but Isaiah 11.2 is the only LXX text where 'spirit' and 'God' both occur with the verb 'to rest'. It is introduced by 'because', suggesting that the allusion (Elliott calls it a quotation) was deliberate and has resulted in a rather cumbersome set of genitives ('of . . . of . . . of'). On this occasion, the author of 1 Peter appears to have changed 'Lord' to 'God', probably because Christ is mentioned in the first phrase.

In summary, the author of 1 Peter uses Isaiah to speak about Christ, the gospel message and the Church. The main passage for understanding Christ is a close reading of Isaiah 53, which is understood as speaking about Christ's non-retaliation in the face of abuse and his redemptive death on behalf of the straying sheep. The gospel message is compared with the imperishable word of God in Isaiah 40.6–8 and given specific content from Isaiah 53, namely, the forgiveness of sins and healing or restoration. The Church is described using a number of epithets originally applied to Israel. Isaiah contributes the promise that the Spirit of God will rest upon them (Isa. 11.2); their vocation to reverence the Lord instead of giving way to fear (Isa. 8.12–13); and their mission to proclaim the mighty acts of God (Isa. 43.21). It is possible that the reference to 'exiles' in the opening verse (1 Pet. 1.1) and to 'aliens and exiles' in 1 Peter 2.11 is intended to evoke Isaiah's 'New Exodus' theme, as has been argued for Luke–Acts, and the explicit quotation from Isaiah 40 could be used to support it. However, neither of these terms occur in Isaiah and if a specific text is intended, Genesis 23.4 is the most likely, where Abraham says to the Hittites, 'I am a *stranger* and an *alien* residing among you.' It seems more likely that 'exile' and 'exodus' were common themes in biblical writings (technically known as *topoi*) and not frameworks that *control* the author's meaning. What is clear is that the author of 1 Peter favours Isaiah over Psalms, whereas the opposite was the case in the early speeches in Acts.

1 Peter and Proverbs

As well as the promise that bearing unjust suffering will lead to blessing (1 Pet. 3.14) and glory (1 Pet. 4.13), the author reminds his readers that the coming judgement will 'begin with the household of God' (1 Pet. 4.17a). He then reflects that 'if it begins with us, what will be the end for those who do not obey the gospel of God?' (1 Pet. 4.17b). The answer is given in the form of a verbatim quotation from the LXX of Proverbs 11.31: 'If it is hard for the righteous to be saved, what will become of the ungodly and the sinners?' (1 Pet. 5.18). The Masoretic Hebrew text says something quite different and would not have supported his argument ('If the righteous are repaid on earth, how much more the wicked and the sinner!'). The LXX either represents a modification of this or is following a different Hebrew text.

In the exhortation of 1 Peter 5.5–6, there is a quotation from Proverbs 3.34 that 'God opposes the proud, but gives grace to

Table 2.5

1 Peter 5.5–6	James 4.6
And all of you must clothe yourselves with humility in your dealings with one another, for *'God opposes the proud, but gives grace to the humble.'* *Humble* yourselves therefore under the mighty hand of God, so that he may exalt you in due time.	But he gives all the more grace; therefore it says, *'God opposes the proud, but gives grace to the humble.'* Submit yourselves therefore to God. Resist the devil, and he will flee from you.

the humble'. This is also quoted in James 4.6 (see Table 2.5) and according to Eugene Boring, 'shows that it had become an element in stock Christian tradition'.[15] Perhaps it suggested itself to the early Church because the LXX rendered the Hebrew word for 'favour' with *charis* ('grace'), a word that had become important for Christians. Thus James 4.6 reads, 'But he gives all the more grace; therefore it says, "God opposes the proud, but gives grace to the humble."' Peter does not have this emphasis but focuses on showing humility to one another. However, it is clear that they are drawing on common traditions, since they both follow the quotation with an exhortation to 'humble' or 'submit' to God, with a positive consequence (he may exalt you/the devil will flee from you). The exhortation in 1 Peter picks up the language of the quotation, that God gives grace to the humble.

1 Peter and the law

Leviticus 19.2

There is only one quotation from the law in 1 Peter (Lev. 19.2), but as it is the first quotation in the letter (1 Pet. 1.16), it is likely to be important. It comes from the same chapter as the command to love one's neighbour (Lev. 19.18), which is quoted extensively in the New Testament, and is the command to be holy as God is holy. It belongs to that section of Leviticus that scholars call the 'Holiness Code' (Lev. 17—26) and Selwyn deduces from this that the author understands the Church as a 'neo-Levitical community, at once sacerdotal and sacrificial'.[16] On the other hand, although much of Leviticus is aimed at the priests, this particular section is aimed at the whole people of God. It is thus truer to say that the parallel is between Israel and the Church, though the focus is certainly on its priestly nature. As we have seen throughout this study, the author has no difficulty applying statements that were originally addressed to Israel to the Church. Holiness was a characteristic of the old covenant and it is equally a characteristic of the new, even if there is less emphasis on ritual requirements.[17]

In the days of Noah

In an extremely difficult passage, the author claims that after Christ's death, he was 'made alive in the spirit, in which also he went and made a proclamation to the spirits in prison' (1 Pet. 3.19). If this is read in conjunction with 1 Peter 4.6 ('the gospel was proclaimed even to the dead, so that, though they had been judged in the flesh as everyone is judged, they might live in the spirit as God does'), it suggests that the imprisoned spirits are the souls of the dead – perhaps those who lived before Christ – who are now given a chance to respond to the gospel. The theory that Christ 'descended into hell' is well known in the second century CE and was included as an article of belief in the Apostles' Creed, though not in the Nicene Creed. Among modern scholars, this interpretation is defended by Goppelt.[18]

However, in 1 Peter 3.20, the imprisoned spirits are identified as those 'who in former times did not obey, when God waited patiently *in the days of Noah*, during the building of the ark, in which a few, that is, eight people, were saved through water'. Since it is very difficult to understand why only this group of sinners is singled out, an alternative suggestion is that the imprisoned spirits are not dead people but 'spiritual beings'. More specifically, they are the 'sons of God' mentioned in the introduction to the flood story (Gen. 6.2), who had sex with human women and begat a race of giants. Not surprisingly, this enigmatic statement was subject to much speculation and in *1 Enoch* they are identified as 'fallen angels' who had been cast out of heaven because of their rebellion (cf. Rev. 12.9). On this view, the proclamation is not the offer of salvation but the confirmation of Christ's victory over the 'spirits' that lie behind human wickedness.[19]

The Enoch literature

The story of Enoch being taken up by God (Gen. 5.24) was subject to much speculation and gave rise to a corpus of writings which describe what he saw on this and subsequent journeys. It includes both cosmology – the nature of the heavenly world – and eschatology – what will happen in the end times. The collection known as *1 Enoch* is only found complete in an Ethiopic translation but fragments have been found in Aramaic, Greek and Latin. It was popular at Qumran, which shows that much of it predates the Christian era and it is indeed quoted in Jude 14–15. It is not quoted in 1 Peter and it is likely that the author is simply drawing on common tradition.[20] *2 Enoch* is known only from late Slavonic manuscripts and is probably several centuries later, while *3 Enoch* is written in Hebrew and is no earlier than the fifth century.[21]

Although the flood represented God's judgement on human wickedness, Noah and his family did survive and so it is not inappropriate to say that they were 'saved through water'. This reminds the author of the waters of baptism, through which his readers have passed, and so he asserts that the flood 'prefigures' Christian baptism. It is not that the flood story predicts Christian baptism but it suggests (or can be seen to suggest) a greater rescue in the future. It is thus an example of typological fulfilment. The author identifies this rescue with the death and resurrection of Christ, which is actualized in Christian baptism.

1 Peter 1.10–12

Before concluding, there is an important passage in 1 Peter 1.10–12 that speaks about the inspiration of prophecy. There are surprisingly few passages like this in the New Testament (1 Cor. 9.9–10; 2 Tim. 3.16; 2 Pet. 1.19–21) and it has therefore been the subject of much debate. I quote it in full, together with some of the key Greek words in italics:

> Concerning this salvation, the prophets who prophesied of the grace that was to be yours made careful search (*exezētēsan*) and inquiry (*exēraunēsan*), inquiring about the person or time (*tina ē poion kairon*) that the Spirit of Christ within them indicated (*edēlou*), when it testified in advance to the sufferings destined for Christ (*ta eis christon pathēmata*) and the subsequent glory [lit. 'glories']. It was revealed to them that they were serving not themselves but you, in regard to the things that have now been announced to you through those who brought you good news by the Holy Spirit sent from heaven – things into which angels long to look!   (1 Peter 1.10–12)

The opening words ('Concerning this salvation') suggest that the subject of the ancient prophecies is not limited to the details of Christ's life, but includes the salvation that he accomplished. This is borne out by the words that follow ('the grace that was to be yours'), which is identified in the last sentence as the good news that was announced to them. Indeed, it was revealed to the prophets 'that they were not serving themselves but you'. However, if the NRSV translation is correct, we also read that their prophecies concerned the 'sufferings destined for Christ and the subsequent glory'. Having read Peter's speeches in

Acts, one naturally takes 'sufferings' and 'glory' to refer to Christ's death and resurrection/exaltation but it is interesting that the word translated 'glory' is in fact plural ('glories') and that he does not use a personal pronoun ('his glory'). It is therefore possible that 'subsequent glories' is not limited to Christ's resurrection/exaltation but refers to the birth of the Church and the reality of salvation. The NIV is open to such an interpretation with its rendering, 'the sufferings of Christ and the glories that would follow'.

Indeed, it is possible that the 'sufferings' could also be a reference to the Church. The debate hinges on the particular Greek phrase (*eis christon*) that is used. The preposition *eis* can indicate purpose and so the meaning could be 'sufferings for the benefit of Christ', that is, those endured by his followers in his name. This is the view of Selwyn ('the sufferings of the Christward road'[22]) and is the reading adopted by the REB ('sufferings in Christ's cause'). Such a meaning would clearly be relevant to the recipients of the letter and arguably does more justice to the plurals ('sufferings'/ 'glories') than a specific reference to Christ.[23]

There are a variety of 'activities' mentioned in this theory of prophecy. First, there is a searching/inquiring activity by the prophets, though nothing is said about what they searched. One of the documents from the Dead Sea Scrolls offers a possible parallel: 'They have neither *inquired* nor *sought* after him concerning his laws that they might know the hidden things' (1QS 5.11). This might suggest the terms refer to some sort of exegetical activity, a view that could be supported by the use of *eraunaō* in John 5.39 ('You *search* the scriptures because you think that in them you have eternal life'). It should be noted that the author of 1 Peter does not state whether their search was successful or not.

Second, there are two verbs ('indicated', 'testified in advance') which belong to the activity of the 'Spirit of Christ'. The first occurs seven times in the New Testament, the two uses in

Hebrews being particularly instructive. In Hebrews 9.8, the laws of the sanctuary are being interpreted: 'By this the Holy Spirit *indicates* that the way into the sanctuary has not yet been disclosed as long as the first tent is still standing.' In Hebrews 12.27, a scriptural text (Hag. 2.6) is quoted and then said to *indicate* 'the removal of what is shaken'. Thus there is ample precedent for seeing 'indicate' as referring to some sort of hermeneutical/discernment activity. The other word ('testified in advance') is a compound word formed by adding the preposition 'before' to the verb 'testify' and is not known before its occurrence in 1 Peter; it was probably coined by the author of 1 Peter himself.

Third, the agent at work within the prophets is said to be the 'Spirit of Christ'. This unusual phrase (only Rom. 8.9; cf. Phil. 1.19) is taken by Anthony Hanson to refer to a specific activity of Christ before his incarnation. He notes that Paul can identify the rock that sustained the Israelites in the wilderness as Christ (1 Cor. 10.4) and thinks that 1 Peter has something similar in mind.[24] However, this seems out of keeping with the use of Scripture in the rest of 1 Peter and is probably just how Christians were in the habit of speaking about the activity of the Spirit in Scripture. Jobes suggests that the effect of using such a phrase points to the unity of what the Spirit said then and what he says now: 'The Spirit who had inspired the prophets was the same Spirit who descended on Jesus at his baptism, identifying him as the Messiah who would experience the foretold sufferings and the glories that would follow'.[25]

Conclusion

Schutter thinks that the prophecy theory in 1 Peter 1.10–12 shows that the author is operating with a 'suffering followed by glory' hermeneutic. He reads texts in the light of the death and resurrection of Christ and therefore finds in them a 'suffering followed by glory' theme, which can be applied to either

Christ or the Church. This is helpful as a general orientation but it is interesting that 'suffering followed by glory' is rarely applied to the same subject. For example, he draws on verses 4, 5, 6, 7, 9 and 12 of Isaiah 53 to show that Christ's suffering and death was of benefit (glory?) to others but he does not use verse 11 ('out of his anguish, he shall see light') to indicate a positive outcome for Christ. On the other hand, he uses Isaiah 11 to encourage his readers that the 'spirit of glory' rests upon them but he does not find a 'suffering' theme in the same passage. Furthermore, it would be difficult to show how the contrast between grass that withers and God's word that abides for ever (Isa. 40.6–8) is being read as 'suffering followed by glory'. His point is not that the grass withers but comes alive the following year; it is a contrast between the transitory and the eternal. Clearly, the author's outlook allows him to apply 'suffering' and 'glory' passages to Christ and the Church but he does not force passages to speak of both when they plainly do not.

Barrett describes Peter's speeches in Acts as 'unreflective' and this could also be applied to 1 Peter. Thus he assumes that texts that were addressed to Israel can be applied to the Church without any need for exegesis or explanation. Indeed, Peter's argument in the Pentecost sermon that David could not have been speaking about himself but a 'Holy One' to come (Acts 2.31) appears to show more hermeneutical awareness than the author of 1 Peter. This is not to say that his use of texts is haphazard or ad hoc. Texts like Isaiah 53 and Psalm 34 are clearly important to him and there are signs of structure and organization in his use of them. But he does not address any of the issues that arise in applying such texts directly to Christ or the Church. Ramsey Michaels says that in this respect, his use of Scripture is a little 'naïve' but Barrett's term ('unreflective') is better. The author of 1 Peter simply assumes that his readers accept that key texts like Isaiah chapters 8, 28, 40 and 53, and key terms like 'chosen people' and 'royal priesthood' speak about Christ or the Church; he does not have to justify such usage.

Finally, does our study contribute anything to the authorship debate? It is interesting that the 'Peter' of Acts primarily uses the Psalms, supplemented by Isaiah, whereas the 'Peter' of 1 Peter focuses on Isaiah, with only a few references to the Psalms. However, it would be impossible to argue that the historical Peter, writing some 30 years later and in very different circumstances, could not have changed his emphasis. After all, Galatians and 2 Corinthians both contain 10 or 11 quotations from Scripture without a single text in common.[26] However, if we turn the argument around, we can say that it is just about impossible to believe that Luke used 1 Peter in order to reconstruct Peter's early preaching. Had he done so, he would surely have made Isaiah central and not attempted to defend the resurrection on the basis of Psalm 16. It would appear that the debate about authorship will have to be argued on other grounds.

3

Jude, 2 Peter and James and Scripture

Introduction

As we saw in the last chapter, some scholars find it difficult to believe that a fisherman like Peter could have written the polished Greek of 1 Peter. However, the difficulties are nothing compared with identifying the author of 2 Peter. Both in terms of content and style, it is hard to imagine the same person writing both works and this also applies to their use of Scripture. In 1 Peter, the use of Scripture is essentially traditional, quoting key psalms (34, 40, 118), key chapters of Isaiah (8, 40, 53) and popular wisdom sayings (Prov. 3.34). The second letter of Peter is quite different, preferring a more allusive style, drawing on books outside the biblical canon (*1 Enoch*, *Testament of Moses*) and showing a particular interest in angels and demons. This is shared with the much shorter work known as Jude and most scholars believe that 2 Peter has used Jude as one of his sources. We will therefore study the shorter work first and then see how it has been used in 2 Peter.[1]

There are also debates about the authorship of James but the traditional view, that it is the work of the brother of Jesus who later became the leader of the Jerusalem church (Acts 15.19), is still well supported.[2] As noted earlier, what has attracted particular interest is his use of Genesis 15.6 ('Abraham believed God, and it was reckoned to him as righteousness') to make a very different point to Paul in Galatians and Romans. According to James 2.24, 'a person is justified by works and not by faith alone'. There are also quotations of Leviticus 19.18 ('Love your neighbour'), two of the Ten Commandments (adultery, murder) and Proverbs 3.34 (grace to the humble). Although James's use of Scripture is not christological in a doctrinal sense, it bears comparison with Jesus' own interpretation of the law, particularly his emphasis on seeing the law in the light of the twin commands to love God and neighbour. But first, we turn to the short letter – only 25 verses – known as Jude.

Jude

After the traditional opening (X to Y, greetings), Jude says that he was intending to write a letter about salvation but now finds it necessary to issue a stark warning: 'For certain intruders have stolen in among you . . . who pervert the grace of our God into licentiousness and deny our only Master and Lord, Jesus Christ' (Jude 4). His response is that their condemnation is certain and he illustrates this by citing a number of previous judgements, drawn from Scripture (the wilderness generation, Sodom and Gomorrah, Cain, Balaam, Korah) or sources outside the canon (angels kept in chains until judgement day, Michael in dispute about the body of Moses). The fact that he weaves these sources together raises interesting questions about how he viewed books like *1 Enoch*, as we shall see also in the book of Revelation.

The biblical characters are not taken in order. He begins with the Exodus, making the point that despite being saved out of Egypt, those who proved unbelieving were destroyed (Jude 5).[3] A similar use of the wilderness rebellion is found in 1 Corinthians 10.1–13 and Hebrews 3.7–13 but neither of these follow it with a statement about the judgement of angels: 'And the angels who did not keep their own position, but left their proper dwelling, he has kept in eternal chains in deepest darkness for the judgement of the great day' (Jude 6). This is also the fate of the intruders, 'for whom the deepest darkness has been reserved for ever' (Jude 13), presumably because they have forsaken their position in the Church. The typology is powerful and in the light of the specific quotation of *1 Enoch* 1.9 in Jude 14–15, it probably derives from such texts as *1 Enoch* 13.1; 14.5; 54.3–5; 56.1–4; 88.1, where the fallen angels are said to be held in chains until the day of judgement. The force of the threat to Jude's opponents depends on such traditions being well known.

The next illustration is 'Sodom and Gomorrah and the surrounding cities', who 'indulged in sexual immorality and pursued unnatural lust' (Jude 7). The Greek terms are not found in the LXX of Genesis 19 but the latter (KJV: 'going after strange flesh') appears to be a deduction from Genesis 19.5, where the men of the city wish to 'know' Lot's angelic visitors. Since Lot offered his female daughters instead, it would appear that the verb 'to know' is being used as a euphemism for sex. However, there is debate as to the nature of their sin. The traditional view is that they wished to have sex with the male visitors, which has given rise to the unfortunate term, 'sodomy'. This is said to explain why Lot offered his daughters instead. However, Richard Bauckham argues that this cannot be the meaning of 'going after strange flesh' and since Jude has just spoken about angels having sex with human women, the most likely explanation is that the men wanted to have sex with Lot's angelic visitors. Thus the offer of his daughters is not because they were female but because they were human. The same parallel between the sin of the fallen angels (known as Watchers) and the sin of the Sodomites is also found in the *Testament of Naphtali* 3.4–5, where they are said to have 'departed from nature's order'.[4]

We then come to the most perplexing of his illustrations. It begins in verse 8 where his opponents are referred to as 'dreamers', probably indicating that they claimed to have special visions, who 'defile the flesh, reject authority, and slander the glorious ones'. It is not stated who these 'glorious ones' are but the implication from what follows is that they are heavenly beings:

But when the archangel Michael contended with the devil and disputed about the body of Moses, he did not dare to bring a condemnation of slander against him, but said, 'The Lord rebuke you!' But these people slander whatever they do not understand, and they are destroyed by those things that, like irrational animals, they know by instinct. (Jude 9–10)

The words, 'The Lord rebuke you!' are taken from Zechariah 3.2, where Satan brings an accusation against the High Priest Joshua (cf. Job 1), but nowhere in the Old Testament is there an angelic dispute about Moses' body. Clement of Alexandria claimed that Jude got the story from the *Assumption of Moses* but no such work has survived under that name. What we do see is a growing tendency in Jewish works to introduce demonic opposition to Old Testament characters. For example, in the Qumran document 4QAmram, Moses' father (Amram) has a dream where the Prince of darkness and the Prince of light argue over his destiny. In the book of *Jubilees*, the devil (called Mastema) is on the side of Pharaoh and the magicians against Moses. And in the *Damascus Rule*, Satan raises up Jannes and his brother to oppose Moses and Aaron (cf. 2 Tim. 3.8). It seems that Jude knew a story that is now only extant in the Slavonic *Life of Moses*, where the devil claimed that Moses' body belongs to him because he was a murderer – a reference to Moses killing the Egyptian in Exodus 2.11–15. Michael opposes him but does not utter the rebuke on his own authority but leaves this to God. As we will see shortly, the author of 2 Peter appears to have found this rather confusing and simply summarizes the point: 'Bold and wilful, they are not afraid to slander the glorious ones, whereas angels, though greater in might and power, do not bring against them a slanderous judgement from the Lord' (2 Pet. 2.10–11).[5]

The following verse continues to illustrate their despicable behaviour by citing three Old Testament rebellions, those of Cain, Balaam and Korah (Jude 11). Cain is of course the first murderer in the Bible but Jewish tradition greatly expanded on the brief account in Genesis. According to Josephus (*Antiquities of the Jews*, 1.52–66), he was guilty of greed and lust and Philo regards him as the ultimate egoist (*That the Worse Attacks the Better*, 32, 78). Balaam does not appear as a bad character in Numbers 22—24 but the reference in Numbers 31.16 ('These women here, on Balaam's advice, made the Israelites act treacherously against the LORD in the affair of Peor') led to the view that Balaam was the cause of the rebellion in Numbers 25.1–3 where 24,000 Israelites died. Since he is described as being with the Midianite kings in Numbers 31.8, rabbinic tradition deduced that he was there to receive his ill-gotten gains. Korah receives a bad press from the start (Num. 16.1–35) and was guilty of instigating a rebellion against Moses and Aaron. It is likely that these illustrations are given as much for their evocative power as for the actual content of their crimes.

We have seen how Jude makes use of traditions from *1 Enoch* and in verse 14 there is a quotation introduced by the words: 'It was also about these that Enoch, in the seventh generation from Adam, prophesied.' The quotation is from *1 Enoch* 1.9, which itself draws on Deuteronomy 33.2, where God is said to be surrounded by 'myriads of holy ones'. Jude seems to have been attracted to the text by its repetition of the word 'ungodly' and he claims that the text is a prophecy about the fate of his 'ungodly' opponents:

> It was also about these that Enoch, in the seventh generation from Adam, prophesied, saying, 'See, the Lord is coming with tens of thousands of his holy ones, to execute judgement on all, and to convict everyone of all the deeds of *ungodliness* that they have committed in such an *ungodly* way, and of all the harsh things that *ungodly* sinners have spoken against him.
>
> (Jude 14–15)

Lastly, it is worth mentioning the admonition at the end of the letter, where Jude says: 'And have mercy on some who are wavering; save others *by snatching them out of the fire*; and have mercy on still others with fear, hating even the *tunic defiled* by their bodies' (Jude 22–23). We have already noted how the phrase 'The LORD rebuke you' comes from Zechariah 3.2 and it is therefore of interest that the verse continues: '"The LORD who has chosen Jerusalem rebuke you! Is not this man a *brand plucked from the fire?*" Now Joshua was dressed in *filthy clothes* as he stood before the angel' (Zech. 3.2b–3). Jude's words are not taken from the LXX but the agreement in sequence (rebuke, plucked from the fire, defiled clothes) makes it likely that the passage is in mind, perhaps combined with Amos 4.11, where a reference to Sodom and Gomorrah is followed by the phrase, 'like a brand snatched from the fire'.[6]

2 Peter

With the exception of a quotation from Proverbs 6.11, the Old Testament material in 2 Peter is mainly that which he found in Jude or was inspired by Jude. For example, he draws on four of Jude's negative examples (angels kept in chains, Sodom and Gomorrah, slandering the glorious ones, Balaam's error), while adding positive references to the salvation of Noah and Lot. He omits the quotation from *1 Enoch* and replaces the obscure reference to Michael's dispute with the devil with a more general comment about angels, perhaps because he did not know the sources of these traditions. It is also interesting that when Jude speaks of 'eternal' punishment (Jude 6, 7) or punishment 'for ever' (Jude 13), 2 Peter only speaks of punishment (2 Pet. 2.4, 6, 17). The result is that 2 Peter is much less sombre than Jude. The extent of their dependence can be seen in the parallels set out in Table 3.1 overleaf.

Noah, Lot and Balaam

After the clause about God not sparing the angels, 2 Peter adds a positive reference to the deliverance of Noah and his family, and after the reference to the destruction of Sodom

Table 3.1

Jude	2 Peter
May mercy, peace, and love *be yours in abundance.* (v. 2)	May grace and peace *be yours in abundance.* (1.2)
For certain intruders have stolen in among you, people who *long ago* were designated for this *condemnation* as ungodly, who pervert the grace of our God into *licentiousness* and *deny our only Master* and Lord, Jesus Christ. (v. 4)	there will be false teachers among you, who will secretly bring in destructive opinions. They will even *deny the Master* who bought them . . . many will follow their *licentious* ways . . . Their *condemnation,* pronounced against them *long ago.* (2.1–3)
And the angels who did not keep their own position, but left their proper dwelling, he has kept in *eternal chains in deepest darkness* for *the judgement* of the great day. (v. 6)	For if God did not spare the angels when they sinned, but cast them into hell (*tartarōsas*[7]) and committed them to *chains of deepest darkness* to be kept until *the judgement.* (2.4)
Likewise, *Sodom and Gomorrah* and the surrounding cities, which, in the same manner as they, indulged in sexual immorality and *pursued unnatural lust,* serve as an example by undergoing a punishment of *eternal* fire. (v. 7)	and if by turning the cities of *Sodom and Gomorrah* to ashes he condemned them to extinction and made them an example of what is coming to the ungodly . . . especially those who indulge their flesh in *depraved lust.* (2.6, 10a)
Yet in the same way these dreamers also defile the flesh, reject authority, and *slander the glorious ones.* (v. 8)	Bold and wilful, they are not afraid to *slander the glorious ones.* (2.10b)
But when the archangel Michael . . . *did not dare to bring a condemnation of slander* against him, but said, 'The Lord rebuke you!' (v. 9)	whereas angels, though greater in might and power, *do not bring against them a slanderous* judgement from the Lord. (2.11)
But these people *slander whatever they do not understand,* and they are destroyed by those things that, *like irrational animals,* they know by *instinct.* (v. 10)	These people, however, are *like irrational animals,* mere creatures of *instinct . . . They slander what they do not understand.* (2.12)

Woe to them! For they go the way of Cain, and abandon themselves to *Balaam's* error for the sake of *gain*, and perish in Korah's rebellion. (v. 11)	They have left the straight road and have gone astray, following the road of *Balaam* son of Bosor, who loved the *wages* of doing wrong, but was rebuked for his own transgression; a speechless donkey spoke with a human voice and restrained the prophet's madness. (2.15–16)
These are *blemishes* on your love-feasts, *while they feast with you* without fear. (v. 12)	They are *blots and blemishes,*[8] revelling in their dissipation *while they feast with you.* (2.13)
They *are waterless* clouds carried along by the winds . . . *for whom the deepest darkness has been reserved for ever.* (vv. 12–13)	These *are waterless* springs and mists driven by a storm; *for them the deepest darkness has been reserved.* (2.17)
'*In the last* time there will be *scoffers, indulging their own* ungodly *lusts.*' (v. 18)	First of all you must understand this, that *in the last* days *scoffers* will come, scoffing and *indulging their own lusts.* (3.3)

and Gomorrah, he adds a reference to the rescue of Lot. Both are called 'righteous' in contrast to the 'ungodly' and allow the author to make the positive point that not only does God know how to 'keep the unrighteous under punishment until the day of judgement', he also knows how to 'rescue the godly from trial' (2 Pet. 2.9). Genesis does not say that Noah embarked on a preaching ministry, but this had become a regular feature in Jewish tradition, with the *Sibylline Oracles* even including one of his sermons (1.148–98). On the other hand, although tradition regarded Lot as righteous (Wisd. 10.6), we do not know of any sources that would account for the statement in 2 Peter 2.8 that Lot 'was tormented in his righteous soul by their lawless deeds'. The language has some similarity to Ezekiel 9.4, where a mark was put on the foreheads of those who 'sigh and groan over all the abominations that are committed in it', a text taken up in Revelation 7.3. However, there is no satisfactory explanation for how the author of 2 Peter connected this with Lot.

Neither is it clear why the author decided to expand the reference to Balaam, first by adding that he loved gain, and second by saying that his madness was restrained by the rebuke of his donkey. It might be because he has just accused the false teachers of behaving like 'irrational animals, mere creatures of instinct' (2 Pet. 2.12) and this reminded him of the story of the donkey in Numbers 22.22–35. But the only madness mentioned in that story is that he beats his donkey because he cannot see the angel barring his way. When he is allowed to see it, he immediately repents and does what the angel says. It is thus likely that 2 Peter is not drawing his additional information from the biblical account – especially as Numbers 22.5 says he is the son of Beor not Bosor – but from other Jewish traditions. The Aramaic paraphrases known as Targums, for example, speak of Balaam's foolishness and Philo says that he died 'stabbed by his own madness' (*On the Change of Names*, 203).

Other scriptural references

The only explicit quotation in 2 Peter occurs in the somewhat distasteful proverb, '"The dog turns back to its own vomit" and, "The sow is washed only to wallow in the mud"' (2 Pet. 2.22). Only the first part is from the Old Testament (Prov. 6.11). The saying about the sow appears to derive from an ancient tradition called the *Story of Ahikar*. The Arabic version runs, 'thou hast been to me like the pig who went into the hot bath with people of quality, and when it came out of the hot bath, it saw a filthy hole and it went down and wallowed in it.'[9] It is possible that the saying from Proverbs suggested the other saying but, given the differences from both the Greek and Hebrew texts,[10] it is more likely that the author of 2 Peter derived them both from a common collection.

In 2 Peter 3, the author seeks to answer a specific accusation of the scoffers: 'Where is the promise of his coming? For ever since our ancestors died, all things continue as they were from the beginning of creation!' (2 Pet. 3.4). His answer is twofold. First, they should understand that everything happens by God's command, as is seen in the creation story ('by the word of God heavens existed long ago and an earth was formed out of water and by means of water') and the flood ('through which the world of that time was deluged with water and perished'). Equally certain is the fact that 'the present heavens and earth have been reserved for fire, being kept until the day of judgement and destruction of the godless' (2 Pet. 3.7). Various texts threaten judgement by fire (Isa. 30.30; 66.15; Mal. 4.1) but in the light of the rest of 2 Peter, it is just as likely that he is drawing on other traditions.

Second, God does not operate with the same timescale as humans for 'with the Lord one day is like a thousand years, and a thousand years are like one day' (2 Pet. 3.8). This draws on Psalm 90.4 ('For a thousand years in your sight are like yesterday when it is past, or like a watch in the night'), which also follows a comment about creation ('Before the mountains were brought forth, or ever you had formed the earth and the world, from everlasting to everlasting you are God' – Ps. 90.2). Ultimately, the author shares the hope of Isaiah that there will be 'new heavens and a new earth, where righteousness is at home' (2 Pet. 3.13/Isa. 65.17; 66.22) but his main point is that this will happen in God's timing. Although he does not speculate on when this will be, the argument suggests that we are dealing with a fairly late document, though how late is debated. For those who continue to maintain Petrine authorship, it would have to be in the early 60s, but the majority of scholars suggest a date in the 90s.

The canon of Scripture

Some Christians find it problematic that Jude appears to regard *1 Enoch* as inspired Scripture and draws freely from other

71

non-canonical sources. Jude is not alone in this. Luke has Paul citing Greek poets in Acts 17.28 and the Jewish tradition (*Sukkah* 3.11) that the rock that miraculously produced water used to follow the Israelites in the wilderness turns up in 1 Corinthians 10.4. The story of two brothers (Jannes and Jambres) opposing Moses in 2 Timothy 3.8 is not found in the Old Testament but occurs in a Qumran document known as the *Damascus Rule* (5.19) and the tradition that the law was given through angels occurs in Acts 7.53 and Galatians 3.19. One way of answering this would be to draw a comparison with the incarnation. Thus just as Jesus was a particular Jewish man with a particular Galilean accent, so Scripture is expressed in the language and thought forms of its various authors, including the texts and traditions known to them.[11] On the other hand, some would argue that a quotation from a work like *1 Enoch* does not necessarily imply that the author regarded the whole work as authoritative; he may simply have discerned truth in the actual words quoted.[12]

James

Although James is best known for his use of Genesis 15.6 to argue that 'a person is justified by works and not by faith alone' (Jas. 2.24), it is important to see this in the light of his rich understanding of the first five books of the Bible. Thus in his discussion of the huge damage that can be done by the tongue, he says that even though 'every species of beast and bird, of reptile and sea creature, can be tamed' (Jas. 3.7), no one can tame the tongue. On its own, this might not be a specific reference to the creation story but two verses later, he says that the tongue curses 'those who are made in the *likeness* of God' (Jas. 3.9). This makes it probable that he has Genesis 1.26 in mind, where God says: 'Let us make humankind in our image, according to our *likeness*; and let them have dominion over the *fish* of the sea, and over the *birds* of the air, and over the *cattle*, and over all the *wild animals* of the earth.' James's point is that although humankind was given dominion over the animal kingdom ('tamed'), it has little control over its own desires and his description of how this leads to death appears to owe something to the Adam and Eve story: 'But one is tempted by one's own desire, being lured and enticed by it; then, when that desire has conceived, it gives birth to sin, and that sin, when it is fully grown, gives birth to death' (Jas. 1.14–15).

Exodus is represented by a discussion of two of the Ten Commandments. James wishes to establish the point that 'whoever keeps the whole law but fails in one point has become accountable for all of it' (Jas. 2.10). He illustrates this by observing that the one who gave the commandment against adultery also gave the commandment against murder (Jas. 2.11). This seems a rather obvious point but Scott McKnight thinks the choice of commandments is deliberate; his opponents are not committing adultery but they are committing murder (Jas. 4.2; 5.6). Most commentators take this figuratively but McKnight thinks it might be more than that: 'Perhaps . . . oppression was leading to the death of poor members of the messianic community, and complicity with the rich on the part of some was contributing to those deaths.'[13] In making such a point, James affirms the unity of the law and the seriousness of transgressing any part of it (cf. Matt. 5.19).

There is a specific quotation of Leviticus 19.18 ('you shall love your neighbour as yourself') in James 2.8, which probably derives from the Jesus tradition (Matt. 5.43; 19.19; 22.39). But what is of particular interest is that just prior to this command, Leviticus is concerned with two things that very much concern James: 'you shall not keep for yourself the wages of a labourer until morning' and 'you shall not be partial to the poor or defer to the great' (Lev. 19.13, 15). The context of James 2.1–7 is precisely that of showing partiality to the rich against the poor and in James 5.4, he issues this warning: 'Listen! The *wages of the labourers* who mowed your fields, *which you kept back* by fraud, cry out, and the cries of the harvesters have reached the ears of the Lord of hosts.' The latter phrase probably draws on Isaiah 5.9 but the warnings of Leviticus 19 are the key text. James is following the teaching of Jesus in elevating Leviticus 19.18 to a hermeneutical principle but, more than any other New Testament writer, he has also drawn on its surrounding context.

There do not appear to be any allusions to Numbers in James but the statement that 'God is one' in James 2.19 ultimately goes back to Deuteronomy 6.4. This was part of the *Shema* ('*Hear, O Israel*') that Jews recited daily, a form of which occurs in the Jesus tradition (Mark 12.29–30). Interestingly, Jesus combined this with Leviticus 19.18 ('love your neighbour') and we find all three elements in James 2: God is one (2.19); love God (2.5); love neighbour (2.8).We might also mention the definition of true religion in James 1.27, which includes looking after 'orphans and widows'. This is a particular concern of Deuteronomy (10.18; 14.29; 16.11; 24.17 etc.), as it was for Jesus (Luke 7.12; 18.3; 21.2).

As well as specific references to the Pentateuch, James has some important things to say about the law. Its importance is clear from the statement that 'whoever keeps the whole law but fails in one point has become accountable for all of it' (Jas. 2.10). Indeed, to criticize the law is to criticize the one who gave the law (Jas. 4.11–12)[14] and to 'hear the law' without actually 'doing the law' is as incongruous as looking in a mirror and immediately forgetting what you look like (Jas. 1.22–24). James's concern is with consistency. Thus if a 'brother or sister is naked and lacks daily food, and one of you says to them, "Go in peace; keep warm and eat your fill", and yet you do not supply their bodily needs, what is the good of that?' (Jas. 2.15–16). From James's point of view, if people are using the slogan 'justification by faith' to indicate that 'works of mercy' are not necessary, they deceive themselves. This was not the teaching of Jesus or the law and so James concludes that 'faith by itself, if it has no works, is dead' (Jas. 2.17).

Finally, before we discuss his controversial claim that 'a person is justified by works and not by faith alone' (Jas. 2.24), it should be noted that, like Jesus and Paul, he can summarize the law in terms of the love command: 'You do well if you really fulfil the royal law according to the scripture, "You shall love your neighbour as yourself"' (Jas. 2.8). The primary meaning of 'royal' here is 'pre-eminent', though it might also carry a connotation of 'kingly' in the sense of pertaining to the kingdom. He can also refer to the law as the 'perfect law' (cf. Ps. 19.7) and the 'law of liberty' (Jas. 1.25), which the NIV renders, 'the perfect law that gives freedom'. Indeed, James says that his readers will be judged by the law that gives liberty/freedom (Jas. 2.12). There is no exact parallel to this expression but the thought comes close to what Paul says in Galatians 5.13: 'For you were called to freedom, brothers and sisters; only do not use your freedom as an opportunity for self-indulgence.' Although the context of James requires him to major on judgement, he can also say – somewhat enigmatically – that 'mercy triumphs over judgement' (Jas. 2.13).

Justification by works

We are now in a position to consider James's scriptural argument that Abraham was justified by works (Jas. 2.14–26). What has perplexed – and sometimes distressed – commentators is that James uses the very same text (Gen. 15.6) that Paul uses in Galatians 3.6 and Romans 4.3 to prove that Abraham was justified by faith and not by works. James's argument runs as follows:

> Do you want to be shown, you senseless person, that faith without works is barren? Was not our ancestor Abraham justified by works when he offered his son Isaac on the altar? You see that faith was active along with his works, and faith was brought to completion by the works. Thus the scripture was fulfilled that says, 'Abraham believed God, and it was reckoned to him as righteousness', and he was called the friend of God. You see that a person is justified by works and not by faith alone. Likewise, was not Rahab the prostitute also justified by works when she

welcomed the messengers and sent them out by another road?
For just as the body without the spirit is dead, so faith without
works is also dead.   (Jas. 2.20–26)

There are three main strategies for understanding this text.
The first thinks that James is contradicting Paul's doctrine of
'justification by faith' and thus relegates it to a minor (Jewish)
voice in the New Testament. The best known example is Martin
Luther, who famously described it as an 'epistle of straw' because
its message was in opposition to 'Paul and all Scripture'.[15]
Although Paul does not specifically mention the sacrifice of
Isaac, his chronological argument in Romans 4 that the promise
of Genesis 15.6 came before the introduction of circumcision
in Genesis 17 would be equally applicable to the offering of
Isaac in Genesis 22. Abraham was declared righteous because
he trusted in God's promise and so it cannot depend on any
later 'work', whether that is submitting to circumcision or his
willingness to offer his only son. However virtuous such 'works'
might be – though the latter would be questioned today – they
are not the basis of the promise in Genesis 15.6.

The second strategy seeks to harmonize Paul and James by
reading James in the light of Paul (already in Calvin). Thus
when James says that 'faith was active along with his works',
what he means is that faith was the guiding force behind his
works. And when he says that 'faith was brought to completion
by the works', what he means is that his faith was thereby shown
to be genuine. Thus there is no contradiction with Paul.
Abraham's actions show that he was guided by faith and in that
sense, one could say that he was 'justified by works', meaning
that his works demonstrated the genuineness of his faith. This
is why he can also use Rahab as an example. The story in Joshua
2 says nothing about her faith but her actions demonstrate
that she was motivated by faith in Israel's God; otherwise
she would have acted in the interests of her own people. Thus
the role of faith is to generate or inspire good works and hence

the analogy at the end of the passage: 'For just as the body without the spirit is dead, so faith without works is also dead' (Jas. 2.26). The spirit energizes the body just as faith energizes good works. Justification can be said to be 'by works' providing that it is understood as those things that demonstrate the presence of faith.

The third strategy is to 'let James be James' and interpret him in light of his own context and traditions. James is clearly close to the teachings of Jesus and so it is somewhat ironic to accuse him of being sub-Christian. Jesus asserted the importance of the law (Matt. 5.17–19), the need to do it as well as hear it (Matt. 7.21–27) and the priority of the love command (Matt. 22.39). Paul's comments in Galatians 3—4 and Romans 4 derive from a particular context where Jewish Christians were forcing Gentile converts to be circumcised. Outside of that context, Paul can also assert the importance of the law (Rom. 7.12), the need to do it as well as hear it (Rom. 2.13) and the priority of the love command (Rom. 13.9). James is not faced with the problem of Gentile circumcision but the problem of those who profess faith but act in ways that are thoroughly inconsistent with it.

This is why he chooses Abraham as an example and in particular, his willingness to sacrifice Isaac. The incident is not taken up in the Old Testament but became a prominent theme in Jewish tradition. Known by the Hebrew word for the 'binding (*aqedah*) of Isaac', it was the key incident that defined Abraham as righteous before God. Thus in the additional books found in the LXX, Sirach 44.19–20 says of Abraham that 'no one has been found like him in glory' and that 'when he was tested he proved faithful'. The author of 1 Maccabees even connects the incident with the promise of Genesis 15.6:

> Remember the deeds of the ancestors, which they did in their generations; and you will receive great honour and an everlasting name. Was not Abraham found faithful when tested, and it was reckoned to him as righteousness? (1 Macc. 2.51–52)

James makes the same connection. Abraham's willingness to sacrifice Isaac constitutes both his faithfulness *and* his righteousness. Now it could be argued that this also fits with the second strategy, where Abraham's faith was shown to be genuine by his willingness to sacrifice Isaac, but James's stress on 'works' counts against this. The two expressions, 'faith was active along with his works' and 'faith was brought to completion by the works', suggest that 'works' are not simply the *product* of faith but a necessary constituent in order to bring faith to completion. As Patrick Hartin says: 'Faith comes to completion through one's actions; and faith expresses the fullness of a righteous relationship with God through actions.'[16] That is why, for James, it is simply impossible to speak about faith without also speaking about works – as indeed it was for Jesus.

Wisdom

We have already mentioned the use of Proverbs 3.34 in James 4.6b ('God opposes the proud, but gives grace to the humble') in our discussion of 1 Peter 5.5–6, where both appear to be drawing on common tradition. But James's dependence on wisdom traditions goes far beyond this one explicit quotation. Indeed, Robert Wall entitles his commentary, *Community of the Wise: The Letter of James.*[17] Consider the following parallels with Proverbs as shown in Table 3.2.

The first two are reminiscent of Jesus' teaching. In the Sermon on the Mount, Jesus says to his hearers, 'Ask, and it will be given to you' (Matt. 7.7). In this case, James is closer to Proverbs since Jesus is not specifically referring to 'wisdom'. However, in the second example, James is closer to the parable of the man who wished to build bigger and bigger barns for his crops, not knowing that this might be the day he dies (Luke 12.16–21), for the context of Proverbs 27.1 is not material gain. The third example does not appear to have a parallel in Jesus' teaching but is close to 1 Peter 4.8, where 'love covers a multitude of sins'. It is possible that both texts drew independently on

Table 3.2

James	Proverbs
If any of you is lacking in *wisdom*, ask God, who gives to all generously and ungrudgingly, and it will be given you. (1.5)	if you indeed cry out for insight, and raise your voice for understanding . . . then you will understand the fear of the LORD and find the knowledge of God. For the LORD gives *wisdom*; from his mouth come knowledge and understanding. (2.3–6)
Come now, you who say, 'Today or *tomorrow* we will go to such and such a town and spend a year there, doing business and making money.' Yet *you do not even know what tomorrow will bring.* (4.13–14)	Do not boast about *tomorrow*, for *you do not know* *what* a day *may bring.* (27.1)
whoever brings back a sinner from wandering will save the sinner's soul from death and will *cover* a multitude of *sins*. (5.20)	Hatred stirs up strife, but love *covers* all offences. (10.12)

Proverbs 10.12 but in the light of the common use of Proverbs 3.34 and the use of the word 'multitude', it probably belongs to Christian tradition.

James also draws on other wisdom books, such as Sirach and the Wisdom of Solomon. For example, in James 1.13, readers are told not to blame God when they are tempted for 'God cannot be tempted with evil and he himself tempts no one'. This appears to draw on the discussion in Sirach 15.11–20, where readers are urged to take responsibility for their actions: 'Do not say, "It was the Lord's doing that I fell away"; for he does not do what he hates. Do not say, "It was he who led me astray"; for he has no need of the sinful.' Other examples can be found in James 1.19 (Sir. 5.11; Eccles. 5.1); 4.11 (Wisd. 1.11); 5.6 (Wisd. 2.12).

Prophets

James draws relatively little from the Prophets, despite urging his readers to consider their suffering and patience (Jas. 5.10). We have noted that the phrase, 'ears of the Lord of hosts' (Jas. 5.4), might be borrowed from Isaiah 5.9, especially as the context is about exploiting the poor through joining 'house to house' and 'field to field'. A more definite allusion occurs in James 1.10–11, where the fate of the rich is compared with the flower of the field which withers and falls under the scorching heat of the sun. This draws on Isaiah 40.6–8 but unlike 1 Peter 1.24–25, he is not trying to make the doctrinal point that God's word abides for ever; it is an illustration that 'in the midst of a busy life, they will wither away' (Jas. 1.11). And Isaiah 32.17 ('The effect of righteousness will be peace, and the result of righteousness, quietness and trust for ever') might lie behind James 3.18 ('And a harvest of righteousness is sown in peace for those who make peace').[18]

Lastly, we might mention the example of Elijah's powerful prayer that prevented rain for three and a half years, which closes the book (Jas. 5.17–18). The story does not come from the prophetic books but 1 Kings 17—18 and in some ways this is indicative of James's use of Scripture. He is not much interested in fulfilled prophecy but is greatly interested in law and wisdom. In sharing with Paul the use of Genesis 15.6 and with 1 Peter the use of Proverbs 3.34, we might reasonably describe his use of Scripture as 'traditional'. But the word takes on a particular significance for James, for not only does he draw on Christian tradition, he also draws extensively on the teachings of Jesus. Thus while he does not offer a christological interpretation of Scripture, he certainly offers a 'Jesus-centred' interpretation.

4

Hebrews and Scripture

Introduction

The Letter to the Hebrews contains around 37 explicit quotations, drawn mainly from the Psalms (16) and the Pentateuch (13), with comparatively few from the Prophets (6). In the light of the rest of the New Testament, it is surprising that there is only one quotation from Isaiah, albeit split into two parts (Isa. 8.17–18/Heb. 2.13). On the other hand, there are some particularly long quotations (Jer. 31.31–34; Ps. 95.7–11) which are repeated in summary form, together with some quotations that occur more than once (Ps. 2.7; 110.4). Thus if we were to proportion the quotations in terms of the number of words, it would look like this: Psalms (47 per cent); Prophets (32 per cent); Pentateuch (18 per cent); 2 Samuel and Proverbs (3 per cent). The Psalms are clearly important to the author and have been the subject of a number of studies.[1] The author, however, despite the ascription to the apostle Paul in the King James Version, is unnamed and remains unknown.[2]

It is clear from the opening words of the book that the interpretation of Scripture is a significant theme for the author: 'Long ago God spoke to our ancestors in many and various ways by the prophets, but in these last days he has spoken to us by a Son' (Heb. 1.1–2a). The statement affirms continuity, for it is the same God who spoke to our ancestors (lit. 'fathers') who has spoken to us. The Scriptures are revelation because they are a record of God *speaking* to his people. But there is also a contrast. In the past God spoke *by the prophets* but now he has spoken *by a son*. One might have expected 'the son' but the indefinite reference focuses attention on the qualitative difference between *prophet* and *son*. The implication is that revelation received 'in these last days' is superior to what has gone before because it comes from a more intimate source. What is less clear is whether the 'many and various ways' that God spoke to the people of old is intended as a contrast to the singular way that God has spoken through his son. The NRSV is fairly neutral but other versions use terms like 'fragmentary' (NEB) or 'partial' (NAB), which could carry a negative connotation. We will reserve judgement until we have seen how Scripture is actually used in the book but this is Graham Hughes's summary of the book's opening:

> [T]he revelation of the Word of God is seen as a continuous activity, stretching right across the boundaries of its various economies, and binding the members of the covenants into a single history of salvation. At the same time it is abundantly clear that in its dispensation through the Son it has achieved a clarity and finality not possible for those who received it through Moses.[3]

Hebrews 1.5–14

Hebrews is unique in the New Testament for immediately launching in to a long series of quotations (known as a catena) linked only by a few brief phrases or questions. On the surface at least, the purpose of the collection is to support the author's assertion announced in Hebrews 1.4, that Jesus is superior to the angels. He does this in three ways. In Hebrews 1.5–6 and 1.13, he asks rhetorically whether God ever said to an angel such exalted things as 'You are my Son' (Ps. 2.7); 'I will be his Father, and he will be my Son' (2 Sam. 7.14); 'Let all God's angels worship him' (Deut. 32.43); and 'Sit at my right hand' (Ps. 110.1). What stands out about these verses is that they are all quoted elsewhere in the New Testament.[4]

The author appears to be consciously building on accepted tradition, perhaps as a platform for introducing his own insights.

In Hebrews 1.8–12, he quotes Psalm 45.6–7 ('Your throne, O God, is for ever and ever . . .') and Psalm 102.25–27 ('In the beginning, Lord, you founded the earth') and claims that they are addressed to the Son. These seem to be his own discovery and are not quoted elsewhere in the New Testament. Finally, in Hebrews 1.7, he quotes Psalm 104.4 to show that angels are simply God's messengers, concluding the collection with the rhetorical question: 'Are not all angels spirits in the divine service, sent to serve for the sake of those who are to inherit salvation?' (Heb. 1.14).

In terms of structure, the collection begins and ends with a messianic promise ('You are my Son'/ 'Sit at my right hand'). The central text comes from Psalm 45.6–7, which presents a number of difficulties. It is clearly addressing the king in verse 7 ('God, your God, has anointed you with the oil of gladness beyond your companions') but appears to address God directly in verse 6 ('Your throne, O God, endures for ever and ever'). It is possible to avoid this difficulty if *elohim* ('God') is taken as an adjective ('Your divine throne' – so RSV) and then we would have messianic promises at the beginning, middle and end of the collection. But since the divinity of the son has already been asserted in Hebrews 1.3 ('He is the reflection of God's glory and the exact imprint of God's very being') and the next quotation in the catena is from Psalm 104.4, which addresses God directly ('In the beginning, Lord'), it is likely that the author not only wishes to preserve the ambiguity of the original but to make positive use of it: Jesus is both the fulfilment of messianic promises and shares God's divinity. Thus Herbert Bateman argues that the catena revolves around the twin themes of Jesus as Davidic King and Jesus as God, forming what is known as a chiasm or ABCB′A′ pattern:[5]

A The Son's Status as Davidic King (1.5)
  B The Son's Status as God (1.6–7)
    C The Son's Status as Divine Davidic King (1.8–9)
  B′ The Son's Status as God (1.10–12)
A′ The Son's Status as Davidic King (1.13–14)

As Bateman demonstrates, the author's exegesis has parallels in rabbinic and Qumran literature but it does raise a number of issues. First, the point that God has never used such exalted language of angels would seem to be contradicted by Genesis 6.2, where they are called 'sons of God', and Psalm 82.6, where they are called 'gods' (the verse quoted in John 10.34). In defence, one might say that these are both plural references and that no individual angel is ever called 'Son' or 'God' in Scripture. Second, on any straightforward reading of Psalm 104.4, the Psalmist is clearly addressing God ('you founded the earth') not Jesus. Similarly, Psalm 45.1 specifically states, 'I address my verses to the king', which is confirmed by the next line, 'You are the most handsome of men.' How then can the author claim that these verses are addressed to the Son? Indeed, the only quotation that specifically compares the Son with angels ('Let all God's angels worship him') is not only missing from the Hebrew text of Deuteronomy 32.43 but reads in the LXX, 'Let all sons of God worship him.'[6] It is not a problem taking 'sons of God' to mean 'angels' and the author might have been influenced by Psalm 97.7, where the Hebrew ('all gods bow down') was rendered by the LXX, 'all his angels bow down'. But the 'him' of both Deuteronomy 32.43 and Psalm 97.7 refers to God, not the Son.

One explanation is that the author of Hebrews did not select these texts for himself but used an already existing collection. Hugh Montefiore thinks the collection was obviously designed for another purpose since 'angels' are only mentioned in one of the quotations. He thinks the purpose was to illustrate the various stages of Christ's life. Thus it begins with testimonies to his pre-existence and eternity (Ps. 2.7; 2 Sam. 7.14). It then moves to his incarnation (when angels worshipped him), baptism (Ps. 45.7 speaks of 'anointing'), Pentecost (Ps. 104.4 speaks of winds and fire) and resurrection (Ps. 102.26 speaks of his indestructibility), concluding with the Church's standard proof-text for the ascension, Psalm 110.1 LXX ('Sit at my right hand until I make your enemies a footstool for your feet'). According to Montefiore, the reason that many of the texts appear to have been taken out of context is that the author is using the collection to support a quite different hypothesis, namely, that the Son is superior to the angels.[7]

Few have found this convincing, though Harold Attridge is open to the possibility that some of the quotations may already have been linked prior to Hebrews.[8] The main issue is how to account for those texts that were not already part of Christian tradition (Ps. 45.6–7; 102.25–27; 104.4). Montefiore thinks they are ill-suited to support the Son's superiority over the angels and suggests that they were used to support Jesus' baptism, resurrection and Pentecost. However, we know from Acts that the early Church drew on Psalm 16 to support Jesus' resurrection – there is no evidence of any interest in Psalm 102 at all. There is some interest in Psalm 104.12 (birds finding habitation and the parable of the mustard seed) but the link with Pentecost is never made. Indeed, the quotation speaks of angels/messengers as God's servants and so is very relevant to the author's argument. This leaves Psalm 45. There is a possible allusion in Luke 1.49 but otherwise the early Church seems to have ignored it. Of course one can speculate that the reference to anointing *could* have been used to support Jesus' baptism but there is no evidence that anyone did. It is just as likely that the author of Hebrews was drawn to the text because the messiah king is addressed as a divine being (or is open to such an interpretation).

Hughes offers criticism from a different perspective. He notes that Hebrews 2.1 tells us the purpose of the catena, namely to 'pay greater attention to what we have heard, so that we do not drift away from it'. The readers already believe that Jesus is God's Son (Ps. 2.7; 2 Sam. 7.14) and is seated at God's right hand (Ps. 110.1). The author is simply bringing in other texts to fill out the statement in the opening verses, that creation was through Jesus and that he is heir of all things. Thus for Hughes, the emphasis on angels is not because some of the congregation were identifying Christ with an angel but because Jewish tradition thought that the law was put into effect by angels (Gal. 3.19; Acts 7.53). The author of Hebrews will go on to show that Jesus is superior to Moses, the human agent of the law (Heb. 3) and the priesthood, the system prescribed by the law (Heb. 5—7). If his purpose was simply to show that Jesus is superior to the angels, he would hardly need to go on and show that he is also superior to Moses or the priests. But if his purpose was to show that the *revelation* that comes through Jesus is superior to that which came through the prophets (Moses is regarded as a prophet), then his argument makes more sense.

Nevertheless, there is still the question of why the author has focused on texts which are either addressed to God or spoken by God and applied them to Jesus. Drawing on the work of Alexander Samely and other rabbinic scholars, Susan Docherty notes that the rabbis were often drawn to texts which contained first-person speech, especially if the speaker was not named. Thus the debate in Mark 12.35–37 about the identity of 'the Lord' in the opening words of Psalm 110.1 ('The Lord said to *my* Lord') is quite plausible in a Jewish setting and is not necessarily a case of imposing a christological interpretation (there is no attempt to identify Jesus as the 'Lord' of the psalm). Similarly, the identity of the 'son' addressed in Psalm 2 or the 'king' addressed as God in Psalm 45 are genuine exegetical questions. The frequency of first-person speech in the Psalms is probably why they figure so much in Hebrews and it is likely that the author understood them as divine speech between Father and Son. Paradoxically to us, the author appears to believe that texts can be 'excerpted from their context' and read in isolation, as well as being part of an interconnected whole, so that the links created between 'originally separate and independent passages of scripture' can speak in unison:

> The author of Hebrews as much as any ancient Jewish exegete . . . regarded it as legitimate interpretation to seek out what scriptural texts imply as much as what they actually say, presumably believing that the new meaning he gave them was inherent in the original revelation, which he regarded as having endless depths of meaning and real contemporary relevance.[9]

Hebrews 2.6–13

If the quotations in chapter 1 are largely allowed to speak for themselves, the words of Psalm 8.4–6 in Hebrews 2.6–8 are subject to exposition. The introduction picks up the thought of the last quotation (Ps. 110.1) that the subjection of enemies has never been promised to angels but with an important addition: 'Now God did not subject the coming world, about which we are speaking, to angels' (Heb. 2.5). This is significant because when read on its own terms, Psalm 8 is indeed speaking about this world: it is a reflection on the creation story where humankind was created 'a little lower' than God but given 'dominion' over 'all things'. However, the text quoted in Hebrews 2.6–8 differs from the Hebrew psalm in two respects: there is a temporal aspect that humankind was made lower 'for a little while' and that it was made lower than the 'angels' rather than 'God':[10]

> What are human beings that you are mindful of them,
> or mortals, that you care for them?
> You have made them *for a little while* lower than the *angels*;
> you have crowned them with glory and honour,
> subjecting all things under their feet.
>
> (Hebrews 2.6–8 NRSV)

These changes allow the author to make a contrast: 'As it is, we do not yet see everything in subjection to them, but we do see Jesus' (Heb. 2.8b–9a). The implication appears to be that one day everything will be subject to humankind, including angels. In the meantime, we take heart that Jesus, who was also made lower than angels 'for a little while', has been crowned with glory and honour. This is known as the anthropological interpretation, where the 'problem' being addressed is the discrepancy between the present experience of humankind and what is asserted in the psalm. However, most scholars think that the NRSV's desire to avoid gendered language ('man', 'son of man', 'him'), however laudable in general, is quite misleading in this case. The same words in the NIV read:

> What is *man* that you are mindful of *him*,
> the *son of man* that you care for *him*?
> You made *him* a little lower than the angels;
> you crowned *him* with glory and honour
> and put everything under *his* feet.
>
> (Hebrews 2.6–8 NIV)

There is debate as to whether readers would have linked 'son of man' with the title used in the Gospels, especially as the Greek lacks the definite article ('the Son of Man'), but the important point is the use of the singular. Having just been told that the promise of subjection of enemies (underfoot) in Psalm 110.1 has never been applied to an angel but (by implication) to the Son, why would the author now wish to state that subjection (underfoot) was in fact given to humankind at creation? It seems more likely that readers would assume that the 'man'/'him' of the psalm is also a reference to the Son, especially as the words, 'You made him a little lower than angels', could easily be taken as a reference to the incarnation. Thus according to George Guthrie, what we have here is a classic example of rabbinic exegesis where two texts that appear to contradict one another are resolved: Psalm 110.1 says that the subjugation of the Messiah's enemies is in the future, while Psalm 8.4–6 says it is a present fact.[11] They are resolved in what follows:

Yet at present we do not see everything subject to him. But we see Jesus, who was made a little lower than the angels, *now crowned with glory and honour* because he suffered death, so that by the grace of God he might taste death for everyone.

(Hebrews 2.8–9 NIV)

This is the christological interpretation, which applies the 'vocation' of humankind in the psalm to Jesus, the representative of humankind. Thus the phrase, 'But we see Jesus', is not intended as a contrast to humankind's present condition but is connected to what follows. We do not yet see everything in subjection to Jesus (as in Ps. 110.1) but we are assured of its truth because we see a figure who has been crowned with glory and honour (as in Ps. 8.4–6), having tasted death for everyone.

A weakness of this interpretation is that the author appears to be solving a problem of his own making. Having quoted a series of texts in chapter 1 to show that the Son is superior to the angels, his christological interpretation of Psalm 8.4–6 has produced a text which now asserts that Jesus was made lower than the angels. It then becomes fortuitous that the LXX rendered the phrase 'a little lower' with an adjective (*brachus*) that can also refer to a short interval of time (cf. Luke 22.58).[12] A possible explanation is that Psalm 8 was already being interpreted christologically in the early Church (1 Cor. 15.27; Eph. 1.22) and so its interpretation was in need of clarification. However, it is by no means clear from these verses that anyone saw a contradiction between the two psalms. It may be that the author saw the opportunity of using Psalm 8 to speak about Christ's humiliation as well as his enthronement.

The quotations that follow in Hebrews 2.12–13 emphasize the solidarity between Christ and his people and may suggest that the anthropological and christological interpretations of Psalm 8.4–6 are not mutually exclusive. The introduction states that 'Jesus is not ashamed to call them brothers and sisters' (Heb. 2.11) and is supported by the words of Psalm 22.22

('I will proclaim your name to my brothers and sisters, in the midst of the congregation I will praise you' – Heb. 2.12). Psalm 22 is used extensively in the Gospel passion narratives and like the cry from the cross in Mark 15.34 ('My God, my God, why have you forsaken me?'), the words are understood as Christ's words. It is unclear if the author sees specific significance in the 'praising and proclaiming' of the quotation but the fact that it is done 'in the midst of the congregation' supports his point – he is one of us.

It is followed by a quotation of Isaiah 8.17b–18a, which is split in two by the word 'again': '"I will put my trust in him." And again, "Here am I and the children whom God has given me"' (Heb. 2.13). As with the psalm, the quotation speaks of an activity of the speaker ('trusting') and solidarity with his people. The passage is not quoted elsewhere in the New Testament or indeed anywhere in Jewish literature but its proximity to the famous 'stone' passage (Isa. 8.14 quoted in Rom. 9.33 and 1 Pet. 2.8) might be the reason for its choice. This is now the third example where the author quotes from a different part of a text that is quoted in the New Testament (Deut. 32; Ps. 22; Isa. 8) – and the extensive use of Psalm 110.4 in Hebrews 5—7 will offer a further example.

Psalm 95.7–11 in Hebrews 3—4

Chapter 3 opens with a paragraph that begins with a parallel between Jesus and Moses (they were both faithful over God's house) followed by a contrast ('Jesus is worthy of more glory than Moses'). The passage draws on Numbers 12.6–8, where God rebukes Aaron and Miriam for criticizing Moses, declaring that 'my servant Moses . . . is entrusted with all my house. With him I speak face to face – clearly, not in riddles; and he beholds the form [LXX "glory"] of the LORD'. The author does not wish to denigrate Moses (see Heb. 11.23–28) but as in Hebrews 3.1–4, he sets up a contrast: Moses was God's servant,

Jesus is God's son. He is thus worthy of more glory – perhaps suggesting that Moses only *beheld* God's glory whereas Jesus *shares* it (Heb. 1.3).

He then turns to warning, beginning with a long quotation of Psalm 95.7–11, a psalm that reflects on Israel's wilderness rebellions and the judgement that followed: 'They will not enter my rest.' The exposition repeats the first line of the quotation ('Today, if you hear his voice, do not harden your hearts as in the rebellion' – Heb. 3.15), the final line ('As in my anger I swore, "They shall not enter my rest"' – Heb. 4.3), and then returns to the first line in Hebrews 4.7. Thus the psalm allows the author to issue a stern exhortation to his readers: 'Let us therefore make every effort to enter that rest, so that no one may fall through such disobedience as theirs' (Heb. 4.11).

However, he is not content with using the psalm merely as an example of disobedience. He wants to argue that the 'today' of the psalm is referring to now and the 'rest' is not the promised land but the eschatological future of his readers – providing they remain faithful. The first draws on the fact that the psalm came much later than the wilderness story and so its 'today' cannot refer to that period. But neither does it refer to the period of David, the author of the psalm according to the LXX (but not the Hebrew), because the meaning of the word 'rest' (*katapausin*) is to be understood in terms of God 'resting' (*katepausen*) on the seventh day in Genesis 2.2. The link is further evidence of the author's use of the LXX, since the Hebrew uses quite different words. It was probably inspired by the fact that Psalm 95 belongs to a group of psalms associated with the Sabbath, as well as the reference to God's works in Psalm 95.9.[13] The word-play allows him to assert that the 'rest' spoken about by the psalm is a Sabbath rest (*sabbatismos*), 'a heavenly reality, which God entered upon the completion of creation'.[14] Such a reality remains open for the readers providing that no one falls prey to unbelief or disobedience.

91

Introductory formulae in Hebrews

The different ways that quotations are introduced in Hebrews has been the source of much debate. In the present passage, Psalm 95.7–11 is first introduced as the words of the Holy Spirit (Heb. 3.7) and then the words of David (Heb. 4.7). But Genesis 2.2 is introduced by the vague expression, 'he has somewhere spoken' (RSV), just as Psalm 8 was introduced in Hebrews 2.6 with 'someone has testified somewhere'. Furthermore, having just quoted Genesis 2.2, the author repeats a line from Psalm 95 with the introduction, 'And again in this place it says' (Heb. 4.5). The focus turns to Psalm 110.4 in Hebrews 5—7, which is first introduced by the words, 'he says also in another place' (Heb. 5.6). More generally, commentators have observed that the author prefers verbs of speaking to verbs of writing in his introductions. Some have deduced from this that he was less concerned with the written word and focuses particularly on God speaking to his people. However, it is clear in his exegesis that the precise details of the written words are also of great importance to him.

High Priest like Melchizedek in Hebrews 5.5—7.28

Chapter 4 ends with an exhortation to approach the throne of grace with boldness because Jesus is their High Priest and fully understands their situation. High Priests do not take this role upon themselves and neither did Jesus. He was called by God in the words of Psalm 2.7 ('You are my Son, today I have begotten you') and Psalm 110.4 ('You are a priest for ever, according to the order of Melchizedek'). The phrase immediately before this ('The LORD has sworn and will not change his mind') is not quoted until Hebrews 7.20 but is anticipated in Hebrews 6.13–20. When human beings utter an oath, they swear by one greater than themselves, namely God. But when God utters an oath, he can only swear by himself, as when he said to Abraham, 'I will surely bless you and multiply you' (Heb. 6.14). Hebrews 7 is, then, an exposition of the meeting between

Abraham and Melchizedek (Genesis 14) and its implications for an alternative priesthood.

The exposition makes the following points. First, as is frequent in Jewish exegesis, etymology is used to give meaning to names and titles. Melchizedek comes from two words, *melek* meaning 'king' and *sedek* meaning 'righteousness'; Genesis 14.18 also calls him king of 'Salem', which means 'peace'. Surprisingly, no further use is made of these derivations. Second, since in Genesis 14 Melchizedek simply appears on the scene and then disappears, the author draws the conclusion that, 'Without father, without mother, without genealogy, having neither beginning of days nor end of life, but resembling the Son of God, he remains a priest for ever' (Heb. 7.3). It is not quite clear if this is a claim to pre-existence but it is certainly a claim to an everlasting priesthood. Third, the story of Abraham giving Melchizedek a tenth of his belongings is linked to the regulation that the Levitical priests are to receive a tithe. The argument is as follows: (1) Abraham's gifts to Melchizedek were the equivalent of paying tithes; (2) Levi paid tithes to Melchizedek because Levi was in a sense 'in the loins of his ancestor' at the time; (3) Scripture therefore knows of two priesthoods; (4) Jesus belongs to the priesthood of Melchizedek since he was manifestly not of the tribe of Levi. This is somewhat different from Paul's Adam typology, since the author's main point is not that Christ supersedes or undoes the work of Melchizedek but that he belongs to the same order. Paul Ellingworth calls Melchizedek an 'anti-antitype', since like Jesus, he also 'has no place in the levitical system'.[15]

What are we to make of this exegesis? At first sight it seems fanciful and unconvincing but two factors should be borne in mind. First, as demonstrated by Bateman, the techniques can easily be paralleled in the Qumran literature and later rabbinic exegesis. They might not have agreed with his conclusions but they would not have despised his methods. Second, we know from the Qumran literature (and *1 Enoch*) that the figure of

Melchizedek was already a subject of speculation. The Qumran document known as 11QMelch (*Melchizedek*) speaks of Melchizedek as a heavenly figure who acts as judge at the end times and, by association with Psalm 82.1, is even called *elohim*.

> For this is the moment of the Year of Grace for Melchizedek. [And h]e will, by his strength, judge the holy ones of God, executing judgement as it is written concerning him in the Songs of David, who said, ELOHIM *has taken his place in the divine council; in the midst of the gods he holds judgement.*
>
> (11QMelch 9–10)

Psalm 110 in Hebrews

It is clear that Psalm 110.1 and 4 play a pivotal role in Hebrews. The first verse is quoted or alluded to in chapters 1, 2, 8, 10 and 12, while the fourth verse appears in chapters 2, 3, 5, 6, 7 and 10. This led George Buchanan to suggest that the whole of Hebrews is in fact a Christian homily based on Psalm 110, with the other quotations used to explain or clarify its meaning.[16] The weakness of this view is that the author appears to show no interest in the intervening verses (in italics):

> The LORD says to my lord,
> 'Sit at my right hand until I make your enemies your
> footstool.'
> *The LORD sends out from Zion your mighty sceptre.*
> *Rule in the midst of your foes.*
> *Your people will offer themselves willingly*
> *on the day you lead your forces on the holy mountains.*
> *From the womb of the morning, like dew, your youth will*
> *come to you.*
> The LORD has sworn and will not change his mind,
> 'You are a priest for ever according to the order of
> Melchizedek.'
> *The Lord is at your right hand; he will shatter kings on the*
> *day of his wrath.*

> *He will execute judgement among the nations, filling them*
> *with corpses;*
> *he will shatter heads over the wide earth.*
> *He will drink from the stream by the path; therefore he will*
> *lift up his head.* (Psalm 110)

However, Gert Jordaan and Pieter Nel have recently argued that the *themes* of the intervening verses are 'victory on the day of battle' (vv. 2–3) and 'victory on the day of wrath' (vv. 5–7) and these can be correlated with Hebrews 2—4 and 8—10 respectively, leading to the following structure for Hebrews:[17]

1	Jesus the appointed King superior even to angels
2—4	Jesus in battle for the eternal rest of believers
5—7	Jesus appointed as Priest-King for ever
8—10	Jesus the atonement for God's wrath to believers
11—12	Jesus the victorious King-Priest in glory

It is by no means impossible that the military imagery of the psalm would have been interpreted as Christ's victory through his death and exaltation but it does not answer why there are around 20 recognizable references to Psalm 110.1 and 4 but none to the rest of the psalm. It seems more likely that Hebrews draws on these two verses, just as it draws on specific verses from Psalms 2, 8, 22, 40, 45, 95 and 104.

Jeremiah 31.31–34 in Hebrews 8—10

Because Jesus is a priest for ever and is 'seated at the right hand of the throne of the Majesty in the heavens' (Heb. 8.1), he is the mediator of a better covenant. Why is a better covenant needed? Because Israel did not continue in the old and so God promised a new one through Jeremiah:

> *This is the covenant that I will make with the house of Israel after those days, says the Lord: I will put my laws in their minds, and*

write them on their hearts, and I will be their God, and they shall
be my people. And they shall not teach one another or say to
each other, 'Know the Lord', for they shall all know me, from
the least of them to the greatest. For I will be merciful towards
their iniquities, *and I will remember their sins no more.*

(Hebrews 8.10–12)

This is part of the longest quotation in the New Testament (131
Greek words) and the italicized words are repeated in Hebrews
10.16–18 (38 words), interestingly with 'minds' and 'hearts'
reversed.[18] According to Paul, Jesus spoke of a 'new covenant'
at the last supper (1 Cor. 11.25; cf. Luke 22.20) and there
are possible allusions to Jeremiah 31.31–34 in 2 Corinthians
3.6 ('who has made us competent to be ministers of a *new
covenant*') and Romans 11.27 ('And this is my *covenant* with
them, *when I take away their sins*').[19] But it does not appear to
be present in Mark's version of the supper ('This is my blood
of the covenant, which is poured out for many' – Mark 14.24)
and is not picked up in the rest of the New Testament. Thus
like his use of Psalm 110.4, the author of Hebrews draws on
early Christian tradition but takes it in new directions. The
word 'covenant' (*diathēkē*) occurs 33 times in the New Testament,
17 of them in Hebrews (14 in chapters 8—10).

The quotation is not immediately explained, except to say
that talk of a 'new covenant' implies the previous one is
'obsolete' (Heb. 8.13). What the author wants to say is that
this promised forgiveness comes through the sacrificial death
of Christ. But before he can do that, he needs to establish that
'without the shedding of blood there is no forgiveness of sins'
(Heb. 9.22) and 'it is impossible for the blood of bulls and
goats to take away sins' (Heb. 10.4). Having done that, he can
then assert that Christ has 'offered for all time a single sacrifice
for sins' (Heb. 10.12) and hence the prophecy of Jeremiah
31 has been fulfilled. Ellingworth points out that there is a
parallel here with the way that the author deals with the
theme of Christ's high priesthood, for he first introduces it

in passing, then quotes the key text, confirms it with other texts, discusses its exegesis in detail and then applies it to his readers:[20]

	The Priesthood	*The Covenant*
Introduced in passing	2.17	7.22
Supported by an OT text	5.6	8.8–12
Confirmed by further texts	7.1–6	9.20; 10.5–7
Discussed in detail	7.15–25	10.11–18
Applied to the readers	7.26—8.2	10.19–39

That sacrifices and offerings are to come to an end is confirmed by deduction and quotation. For the author, the sheer repetition of the sacrifices is itself a sign that they are unable to 'make perfect those who approach' (Heb. 10.1) for 'every priest stands day after day at his service, offering again and again the same sacrifices that can never take away sins' (Heb. 10.11). Indeed, the very details of the tabernacle, where Moses was instructed to make everything according to the 'pattern' (*typos*) of what he was shown, indicates that something better was to come. Drawing on ideas found in Philo (and Plato),[21] the earthly tabernacle is but a 'sketch' or 'shadow' of the heavenly reality (Heb. 8.5), just as the law is only a 'shadow of the good things to come and not the true form of these realities' (Heb. 10.1). It is because Christ's sacrifice took place in a *heavenly* sanctuary that it can have eternal consequences. The transitory nature of the sacrificial system is also confirmed by a quotation from Psalm 40.6–8:

'Sacrifices and offerings you have not desired,
but a *body you have prepared for me*;
in burnt-offerings and sin-offerings you have taken
    no pleasure.
Then I said, "See, God, I have come to do your will,
    O God"
(in the scroll of the book it is written of me).'
(Hebrews 10.5–7)

The author of the psalm claims in verse 8, 'I delight to do your will, O my God; your law is within my heart,' which might explain the link with Jeremiah 31. In addition, verse 9 ('I have told the glad news of deliverance in the great congregation') is close to the quotation of Psalm 22.22 in Hebrews 2.12 ('I will proclaim your name to my brothers and sisters, in the midst of the congregation I will praise you'). Once again we have an example of first-person speech understood as words between Christ and God. Martin Karrer not only sees this as an important exegetical principle but also as a contrast with the Gospels: 'the Jesus of Hebrews differs in a double sense from the Jesus of the Gospels. He speaks only words of scripture . . . and he speaks these words relating to his pre-existence.'[22]

There is a textual conundrum in the quotation. According to the NRSV, Psalm 40.6 makes no mention of a 'prepared body' but reads: 'Sacrifice and offering you do not desire, but you have given me an *open ear*.' The last phrase translates two Hebrew words, the noun 'ears' and the verb 'dug out', a graphic description of 'unblocked ears', presumably referring to ears that are 'open' or 'attentive' (the NIV's 'pierced ears' is likely to confuse a modern reader). However, it is likely that the author is simply following the LXX text before him,[23] which also reads 'body', either through a misreading of the Hebrew text or more likely, a deliberate interpretation where a part of something ('ears') is taken as a reference to the whole ('body'), technically known as *pars pro toto*. It has to be said that the author's aim is not primarily to offer a proof-text for the incarnation but to show that the sacrifices offered 'again and again . . . can never take away sins' (Heb. 10.11). But he does draw on the word 'body' when he says: 'And it is by God's will that we have been sanctified through the offering of the *body* of Jesus Christ once for all' (Heb. 10.10). If the author of Hebrews was aware that this differs from the Hebrew text, he would probably have concluded that the LXX was the first stage in making clear the true meaning of the text.

Hebrews 10.19–39

The author's presentation of Christ as High Priest is brought to a close by an impassioned plea for perseverance. They should 'hold fast to the confession of our hope without wavering' (10.23), 'consider how to provoke one another to love' (10.24) while 'encouraging one another, and all the more as you see the Day approaching' (10.25). They are urged to remember their former commitment when they were 'publicly exposed to abuse and persecution' (10.33) and 'cheerfully accepted the plundering' of their possessions. They are also given one of the starkest warnings in the New Testament: Christians who persist in sin are guilty of spurning the Son of God, profaning the blood of the covenant and outraging the Spirit of grace (10.29). They face a punishment more terrible than anything exacted in the law of Moses. The severity is first evoked by an allusion to Isaiah 26.11, where God is asked to consume his adversaries with fire.[24] The implication is that the readers do not want to put themselves in the position of opposing such a God. There is also a reminder of the principle that a verdict rests on the 'testimony of two or three witnesses' (Deut. 17.6; 19.15) and is 'without mercy' (Deut. 13.8). It is possible that the three accusations that follow (spurning . . . profaning . . . outraging) are seen as the three witnesses that confirm the negative verdict.

The warning is completed by quoting two phrases from the 'Song of Moses' in Deuteronomy 32. The first phrase ('vengeance is mine, I will repay') comes from Deuteronomy 32.35 and is also quoted by Paul in Romans 12.19. Paul's use is very different but it is interesting that the form of the text agrees exactly with Hebrews 10.30, but differs from both the LXX and the Hebrew text.[25] It suggests that the author is drawing on early Christian tradition and indeed the 'Song of Moses' was extremely popular in the early Church (cf. Matt. 4.10; Rom. 10.19; 12.19; 15.10; Rev. 15.3–4). The second phrase ('The Lord will judge his people') comes from Deuteronomy 32.36 and the two quotations are linked by 'and again', as in Hebrews 1.5 and 2.13. The application turns on the dual use of the word 'judge' (*krinō*), which can mean 'vindicate', as in Deuteronomy 32.36, or 'punish' as in Hebrews. Attridge calls it a 'tendentious application'[26] though much in Deuteronomy 32 is about punishment. The section ends with the words: 'It is a fearful thing to fall into the hands of the living God' (Heb. 10.31).

Habakkuk 2.3–4 in Hebrews 10.37–38

In Habakkuk 2, God promises a vision that 'will surely come, it will not delay' (Hab. 2.3) and then contrasts the proud whose 'spirit is not right in them' with 'the righteous [who] live by their faith' (Hab. 2.4). The LXX has 'live by *my* faith', presumably in the sense of God's faithfulness. On the surface, this looks like a major change but in reality, living by God's faithfulness means trusting in God's faithfulness, in other words, living by faith. Paul, when he quotes this verse in Romans 1.17 and Galatians 3.11, omits the pronoun altogether, leading to the concise but ambiguous expression, 'the righteous by faith will live'. It is ambiguous because the phrase 'by faith' could modify the noun 'righteous' ('Those who are *righteous by faith* will live') or the verb 'live' ('The righteous will *live by faith*'). Richard Hays thinks that Paul is purposely drawing on both meanings ('righteousness comes by faith' and 'the righteous live by God's faithfulness') but most scholars think that Paul is steering the reader towards the former.[27]

In Hebrews, the first-person pronoun ('my') is retained but there is some doubt as to its position. The best manuscripts place it after 'righteous' ('my righteous one will live by faith') but there is some early evidence for placing it after 'faith' ('the righteous will live by my faithfulness'). The usual explanation for this is that a copyist attempted to conform the reading of Hebrews to the LXX but since we also find the same variations among the LXX manuscripts, it is difficult to be certain.[28]

The first words of the quotation do not come from Habakkuk but appear to draw on Isaiah 26.20. The three words (*micron hoson hoson*) literally mean 'small, as many as many', and are only found in the LXX at Isaiah 26.20 (and repeated in *Odes* 5.20). The initial *eti* ('yet') makes it clear that the reference in Hebrews is to a short space of time, which in Isaiah 26.20 refers to the coming of God's wrath 'to punish the inhabitants of the earth for their iniquity' (Isa. 26.21). It has convincingly been argued that the author was drawn to this text because of its emphasis on the coming of God's wrath, a theme that links his quotations from Psalm 2 ('for his *wrath* is quickly kindled' – v. 11), Psalm 95 ('in my anger/*wrath* I swore, "They shall not enter my rest"' – v. 11) and Psalm 110 ('The Lord is at your right hand; he will shatter kings on the day of his *wrath*' – v. 5). We have already noted his use of Isaiah 26.11 in Hebrews 10.27.

The Hebrew text of Habakkuk 2.3–4 is difficult and in trying to make sense of it, the LXX translator introduced difficulties of his own. In particular, because the word 'vision' is feminine in Greek, two of the masculine words that follow ('wait for *him*' and 'when *he* comes') cannot refer back to the vision, as it does in the Hebrew text, but must refer to a person. The rest of the pronouns are ambiguous and could be either neuter ('it') or masculine ('him'). Thus there are two major ways of reading the LXX. The 'he' is either a rather strange personification of the vision or it refers to a person, perhaps a witness to the vision in the last days or even to the one who will interpret it. This means that God's displeasure is either with the delay of the vision or the witness/interpreter of the vision. Faced with such difficulties, the author of Hebrews adds a definite article to the word 'coming' and thus identifies the figure as 'the coming one' of Christian tradition (Matt. 3.11; 11.3; 21.9), and moves the clause about God's displeasure to the end so that it forms a contrast to those who live by faith (see Table 4.1 overleaf).

Such changes could be seen as 'textual manipulation', a deliberate strategy to derive a meaning which better fits the author's

Table 4.1

Habakkuk 2.3–4 (NRSV)	Habakkuk 2.3–4 (LXX)	Hebrews 10.37–38 (NRSV)
		For yet 'in a very little while,
For there is still a vision for the appointed time; it speaks of the end, and does not lie. If it seems to tarry, wait for it; it will surely come, it will not delay. Look at the proud! Their spirit is not right in them, but the righteous live by their faith.	For there is still a vision for an appointed time, and it/he will rise up at the end and not in vain. If it/he should tarry, wait for *him*, for when *he* comes it/he will come and not delay. If it/he draws back, my soul is not pleased in it/him. but the righteous shall live by my faith.	the one who is coming will come and will not delay; but my righteous one will live by faith. My soul takes no pleasure in anyone who shrinks back.'

argument. However, the complexities of the textual tradition should at least make us pause before settling on such a verdict. Habakkuk's vision is eschatological and asserts that at the end, there will be a division between those who trust and those who do not. This is also the message of Hebrews, although its author has had to work hard with a LXX text which according to Radu Gheorghita, is 'marred by several syntactical and logical inconsistencies'.[29] He concludes that the author's changes are 'not only a legitimate rearrangement of the text intended to untangle the meaning of Hab. 2:2–4 LXX, they are also congruent with and supported by the overall message of the LXX Hab.'.[30]

The cloud of witnesses in Hebrews 11

Similar lists of biblical saints are common in writings between the Testaments (Sirach 44; 1 Maccabees 2; Wisdom 10; Philo) and we have already discussed Stephen's speech in Acts 7 and Paul's speech in Acts 13. In Hebrews 11, most space is given to Abraham (11.8–19) and Moses (11.23–29) but mention is also made of Abel, Enoch, Noah, Isaac, Jacob, Joseph and Rahab. Others are named (Gideon, Barak, Samson, Jephthah, David, Samuel) but the author confesses that he does not have time to elaborate (11.32). The focus is firmly on the hero's faith and he begins with what amounts to a definition:

> Now faith is the assurance of things hoped for, the conviction of things not seen. Indeed, by faith our ancestors received approval. By faith we understand that the worlds were prepared by the word of God, so that what is seen was made from things that are not visible. (Hebrews 11.1–3)

However, as Attridge points out, faith is not explicit in the original stories and has either been deduced by the author or is present in other Jewish traditions. For example, Genesis 4 does not say why God accepted Abel's sacrifice but rejected Cain's. The author claims that it was because Abel was righteous and made his offering in faith (Heb. 11.4). This appears to be based on the author's belief that 'without faith it is impossible to please God' (Heb. 11.6) and since God was evidently pleased with Abel, he must have been a man of faith. That Abel was righteous is attested in Matthew 23.35 ('the blood of righteous Abel') and 1 John 3.12 ('Cain who was from the evil one and murdered his brother. And why did he murder him? Because his own deeds were evil and his brother's righteous'). But Hebrews is unique in attributing faith as the reason for God's acceptance.

Philo on Cain and Abel

Philo uses etymology to deduce that Cain ('possession') is self-serving while Abel ('referring to God') puts God first. He notes that Genesis 4.3 says that Cain brought his offerings 'in the course of time', which he interprets as reluctance, while Abel's offering was immediate, since no such qualification is attached. He also notes that Abel is said to have brought the 'first-born' of his flock, implying the best, whereas no such attribute is said of Cain's offering of 'fruit'. In general, he sees a qualitative difference between the offering of 'inanimate things' and 'living sacrifices' but associates this with character rather than faith. Ultimately, the importance of the story for Philo is that it speaks of the dual nature of human beings: 'For the soul, which destroys out of itself the virtue-loving and God-loving principle, has died as to the life of virtue, so that Abel (which appears a most paradoxical assertion) both is dead and alive. He is dead, indeed, having been slain by the foolish mind, but he lives according to the happy life which is in God' (*That the Worse Attacks the Better*, 1.32).

The author's comments on Abraham have parallels with Acts 7, Romans 4 and James 2 (see Table 4.2) but his particular focus is the *aqedah* or 'binding' of Isaac. As we have seen, this was a prominent theme in Jewish tradition (Sir. 44.20; *Jubilees* 17.15–18; 1 Macc. 2.52) and may lie behind such passages as John 3.16 ('gave his only Son') and Romans 8.32 ('did not withhold his own Son, but gave him up'). What is of particular interest is that both Paul and the author of Hebrews deduce from the Genesis narratives that Abraham believed that God could bring life out of death. For Paul, this comes from Abraham's willingness to believe that God could give a son to parents whose bodies were as good as dead (Rom. 4.19). In Hebrews, having quoted Genesis 21.12 ('It is through Isaac that descendants shall be named after you' – Heb. 11.18), the writer deduces that Abraham's willingness to sacrifice Isaac was because he 'considered the fact that God is able even to raise someone from the dead – and figuratively speaking, he did receive him back' (Heb. 11.19). Abraham not only looked forward to a heavenly home, he also believed in resurrection.

Table 4.2

Hebrews 11	Acts 7	Romans 4	James 2
		Righteous by faith (Gen. 15.6)	Righteous by works (Gen. 15.6)
Left his homeland	Left his homeland		
Stayed in a foreign land	Stayed in a foreign land		
	Received circumcision	Received circumcision	
	Accepted land was not for him		
Believed he and Sarah could have a child		Believed he and Sarah could have a child	
Willing to sacrifice Isaac			Willing to sacrifice Isaac
Sacrifice of Isaac was like believing God can bring life out of death		Birth of Isaac was like believing God can bring life out of death	

The summary of Moses' life has also received enhancements. For example, despite the fact that Exodus 2.14 states that Moses was afraid of the Pharaoh, Hebrews praises him for being 'unafraid of the king's anger' (Heb. 11.27). His identification with the people of Israel is said to have been a choice to share ill-treatment rather than the 'fleeting pleasures of sin'. Josephus uses this same expression to explain why Joseph resisted the charms of Potiphar and so the author is probably drawing on common tradition. Most significant of all, Moses' willingness to suffer with the Israelites is because he 'considered abuse suffered for the Christ to be greater wealth than the treasures of Egypt' (Heb. 11.26). The particular word used for abuse here (*oneidismos*) is found in the LXX of Psalm 69.9 and 89.51 and is associated with the crucifixion in Mark 15.32 and Romans 15.3. Moses not only trusts God by focusing on the future promise, his faith is even said to be 'cruciform' in nature. Thus while the author asserts that certain aspects of the law/covenant are now obsolete (Heb. 8.13), he virtually turns Abraham and Moses into Christians before Christ.

Miscellaneous quotations in Hebrews 12—13

The warnings and exhortations that punctuate the book (Heb. 2.1–4; 3.12–15; 4.11, 16; 5.11—6.12; 10.19–38) are now drawn together in the final two chapters. The author begins with the exhortation to 'run with perseverance the race that is set before us' (Heb. 12.1), an athletic metaphor found in Paul (1 Cor. 9.24–27; Gal. 2.2) and other writings (4 Macc. 17.10–17). His point is that competing involves endurance, discipline and hardship, the same qualities that God requires from his children (lit. 'sons'). This is supported by a quotation from Proverbs 3.11–12, which is introduced by the words, 'And you have forgotten the exhortation that addresses you as children' (Heb. 12.5). We have seen examples of where God or the Spirit is said to speak through Scripture but here Scripture is itself said to speak. The introduction could also be translated as a question ('Have you forgotten . . . ?') but the point is the same – the question is rhetorical and suggests that such teaching was part of their Christian instruction.

The quotation refers to the discipline (*paideia*) that God's children receive, not as a sign of abandonment but as a sign of love. This was commonly thought to entail 'reproach' (Prov. 5.12; Job 5.17) and 'chastisement' (Prov. 13.24; Sir. 22.6), though the NRSV's use of 'punishment' for the former could be misleading. For us, punishment is more about administering justice than character formation and most translations prefer a word like 'rebuke' or 'reprove.'[31] The quotation follows the LXX, which appears to have mistaken the Hebrew phrase 'as a father' for the verb 'chastise' (they have the same consonants), thus eliminating the father/son parallel. This is interesting since Hebrews does likewise but immediately expounds the text in the light of the common experience of 'sons' (NRSV 'children') disciplined by their 'fathers' (NRSV 'parents'). This could suggest that although his quotation follows the LXX, he is aware of the Hebrew text (although it could simply be a deduction from the word 'son').

In contrast to the 'heroes' cited in Hebrews 11, the author urges the readers not to be like Esau, 'an immoral and godless person, who sold his birthright for a single meal' (Heb. 12.16). The adjective 'immoral' (*pornos*) usually refers to sexual sin and the author may be drawing on traditions such as Philo, who spoke of Esau 'indulging without restraint in the pleasures of the belly and the lower lying parts'.[32] Alternatively, his meaning might be a metaphorical reference to apostasy (unfaithfulness to God), especially as he concludes by stating that Esau 'found no chance to repent' (Heb. 12.17). This is not stated in the biblical story (Gen. 27.30–40) but corresponds to the author's view that 'it is impossible to restore again to repentance those who have once been enlightened . . . and then have fallen away' (Heb. 6.4–6). Esau was desperate to change his father's mind but there is no hint of repentance for his former actions. It would appear that the author's understanding of idolatry and repentance for Christians has influenced his reading of the Genesis story.[33]

There is an interesting use of Scripture in Hebrews 12.18–24. The author draws on the Sinai stories to paint an awesome picture of God by describing the scene ('blazing fire, and darkness, and gloom, and a tempest' – Deut. 4.11), the threat ('If even an animal touches the mountain, it shall be stoned to death' – Exod. 19.12–13), the reaction of Moses ('I tremble with fear' – Deut. 9.19) and a statement that 'our God is a consuming fire' (Deut. 4.24). However, the author begins by stating that the readers have not come to something[34] like this; instead, they have come to a place of joy, 'the city of the living God, the heavenly Jerusalem, and to innumerable angels in festal gathering' (Heb. 12.22). But having stated this contrast, he once again draws on the awesome images (adding Hag. 2.6) to issue a warning: 'if they did not escape when they refused the one who warned them on earth, how much less will we escape if we reject the one who warns from heaven!' (Heb. 12.25). Thus he is able to use the awesome images both as a contrast to what awaits the readers and as a warning of what will befall them if they are unfaithful. It is similar to what George DeForest Lord said of Milton, that he 'repeatedly denies the beauty of countless pagan paradises in comparison with Eden, while tacitly employing their strong legendary associations to enhance and embellish its incomparable perfections'.[35]

In Haggai 2.1–9, the prophet is urging those who have returned from exile to rebuild the temple. He encourages them with an oracle that God will 'shake the heavens and the earth', as well as the 'nations, so that the treasure of all nations shall come, and I will fill this house with splendour' (Hag. 2.6). The author of Hebrews only quotes from the first part ('Yet once more I will shake not only the earth but also the heaven') and interprets it eschatologically. The shaking refers to the removal of all that is transitory, leaving a 'kingdom that cannot be shaken' (Heb. 12.28). According to Attridge, Hebrews 'does not seem to suggest, as do some apocalyptists, a renewal of heaven and earth. What is expected is rather the complete destruction of what, because it can be "shaken," is transitory.'[36]

The final quotations occur in chapter 13 and draw on the promise to Joshua that God will never leave or forsake him (Deut. 31.6, 8), and the Psalmist's confidence that since God is with him, he has nothing to fear from anyone else (Ps. 118.6). The application of the promise to Joshua is heightened by changing to the first person ('I will never leave you or forsake you'), which forms the basis ('So we can say with confidence') of appropriating the psalm: 'The Lord is my helper; I will not be afraid. What can anyone do to me' (Heb. 13.6). The author knows that trouble lies ahead and urges them not to shrink back from it ('Let us then go to him outside the camp and bear the abuse he endured' – Heb. 13.13). But they go in the confidence that God is with them, the promises to Joshua and the Psalmist understood as directly addressing their own situation.

Conclusion

We began with a quotation from Hughes to the effect that the author of Hebrews asserts both continuity ('the revelation of the Word of God is a continuous activity, stretching right across the boundaries of its various economies') and difference (the 'dispensation through the Son has achieved a clarity and finality not possible for those who received it through Moses'). We are now in a position to confirm this, for on the one hand, the author speaks of a new covenant, a new priesthood and a better sacrifice. His readers can look forward to the joy of the 'festal gathering' in the 'heavenly Jerusalem' rather than the 'blazing fire' of Mount Sinai. On the other hand, the author can assert that God is a 'consuming fire' and if Israel's disobedience did not go unpunished, it will be far worse for those who disobey the 'one who warns from heaven'. In addition, although stressing the superiority of the new dispensation, the author finds nothing deficient in the faith of the heroes of chapter 11. Indeed, Abraham believed in resurrection and Moses' faith was cruciform in nature.

The author's use of Scripture is grounded in the tradition before him, drawing on well-known texts from Genesis, Deuteronomy, the Psalms and Habakkuk. However, as well as quoting some of the same texts that other New Testament writers quote (Ps. 2.7; 8.6; 110.1; Hab. 2.4), he also draws on neighbouring verses (Ps. 8.4–5; Ps. 110.4; Hab. 2.3). In addition, he does not quote the 'forsaken' saying from Psalm 22.1 (as in Mark and Matthew) but the 'in the midst of the congregation' saying from Psalm 22.22. Similarly, he does not quote the 'stone' saying from Isaiah 8.14 but the 'solidarity with God's people' saying from Isaiah 8.18. Thus while grounded in the early Christian tradition, the author of Hebrews goes considerably beyond it, both extending the tradition and discovering texts of his own.

His quotations are drawn from the LXX, even when this departs significantly from the Hebrew text that has come down to us. Small changes are sometimes needed to adapt the saying to the context and in cases where the differences are significant, as with Habakkuk 2.3–4, this can often be explained by ambiguities in the text. He makes particular use of the Psalms and Docherty is probably correct that their frequent use of the first-person pronoun ('I') is responsible for this. The rabbis also thought that such pronouns required clarification and the author of Hebrews offers it by interpreting words spoken *by* God or addressed *to* God as a divine exchange between God and Jesus. Guthrie is also of the view that many of the techniques used by the author can be paralleled in rabbinic writings, and he sees the apparent contradiction between Psalm 8.6 (everything is subject to the messiah) and Psalm 110.1 (everything *will be* subject to the messiah) as a good example of resolving two apparently contradictory texts. Although few scholars today believe that Hebrews was written by the apostle Paul, it clearly comes from a mind every bit as sharp and knowledgeable of Jewish tradition.

5

Revelation and Scripture

Introduction

The book of Revelation is like no other book in the New Testament. It begins like a letter ('John to the seven churches that are in Asia: Grace to you and peace' – 1.4), and ends like a letter ('The grace of the Lord Jesus be with all the saints. Amen' – 22.21) but instead of the usual body of a letter, it consists almost entirely of visions and oracles. The closest parallel in the New Testament is the eschatological discourse of Jesus (Matthew 24/Mark 13/Luke 21), which predicts the coming of false prophets, a time of persecution and an apocalyptic calamity ('But in those days, after that suffering, the sun will be darkened, and the moon will not give its light, and the stars will be falling from heaven' – Mark 13.24–25). Paul briefly tells the Thessalonians that 'the Lord himself, with a cry of command, with the archangel's call and with the sound of God's trumpet, will descend from heaven' (1 Thess. 4.16) and in his second letter, he adds that before this happens, a 'lawless one' will arise, who 'opposes and exalts himself above every so-called god or object of worship, so that he takes his seat in the temple of God, declaring himself to be God' (2 Thess. 2.3–4).[1] With the exception of the seven messages to the churches in Revelation 2—3, almost all of Revelation consists of apocalyptic material like this.

John does not quote Scripture but his visions allude to numerous biblical passages, so much so that estimates of the actual number range from 250 to well over 1,000. Sometimes particular passages stand out, such as the promise to rule the nations with a rod of iron (Ps. 2.8–9) in Revelation 2.27, 12.5 and 19.15, but usually John weaves together a number of texts to form a richly

111

evocative tableau. For example, in John's inaugural vision (Rev. 1.12–18), there are at least eight identifiable allusions, drawn from Daniel (7.9, 13; 10.5, 6), Ezekiel (1.24; 9.2) and Isaiah (44.6; 49.2). This raises the question of whether the combination of texts is *primarily* rhetorical, to give the hearer (Rev. 1.3) an impression of what John saw, or theological, to convey specific theological meaning by evoking particular texts.[2] Few would doubt that John's use of the messianic promise of Psalm 2.8–9 is intended to convey theological meaning but there is considerable debate about passages like the inaugural vision.

What is the best way of exploring this richly evocative material? One possibility would be to work our way through the book and comment on the allusions as they appear. However, since the allusions are so numerous, this would be tantamount to writing a commentary on the whole book. Alternatively, we could follow the example of a number of scholarly works and focus on John's use of particular Old Testament books, such as Isaiah, Ezekiel, Daniel and Zechariah. This has the advantage of highlighting a number of John's techniques, such as his use of major sections of Ezekiel (chs 1, 9—10, 16—23, 26—27, 37—48) in the same order in Revelation (chs 4, 7—8, 17, 18, 20—22), and his repeated use of Daniel 7 in Revelation 1, 5, 13 and 17. This works well for those who have a good knowledge of Revelation but it is easy to get lost in the details. We will therefore adopt a third approach, which will highlight John's use of Scripture, while also giving the reader a sense of what Revelation is all about. We will thus look at John's use of Scripture under the following five headings: God, Jesus and the Spirit; dragon, beast and false prophet; judgements and disasters; witness and struggle; final salvation.

God, Jesus and the Spirit

After announcing the chain of revelation (God – Jesus – Angel – John) in Revelation 1.1–2 and a blessing on those who hear and keep the 'words of the prophecy' (Rev. 1.3), John offers what appears to be a Trinitarian greeting (Rev. 1.4–5) from God ('who is and who was and who is to come'), the Spirit ('and from the seven spirits who are before his throne') and Jesus ('and from Jesus Christ, the faithful witness, the firstborn of the dead, and the ruler of the kings of the earth'). All three descriptions are based on Old Testament passages. The description of God as the one 'who is and who was and who is to come' is repeated in Revelation 1.8 and in its more logical order in 4.8 ('who was and is and is to come'). It also appears in shortened form (without the future tense) in Revelation 11.17 and 16.5. The title is not found anywhere else in the New Testament and is almost certainly a reflection on Exodus 3.14, where God identifies himself as 'I AM WHO I AM'. This deeply mysterious text, which could also be translated, 'I WILL BE WHAT I WILL BE' (NRSV footnote), was taken up by Isaiah in such affirmations as, 'I am He; I am the first, and I am the last', and in *Targum Pseudo-Jonathan*, which rendered Exodus 3.14 as 'I am he who is and who will be' and Deuteronomy 32.39 as 'I am he who is and who was, and I am he who will be'.[3]

It is somewhat surprising that the Spirit is mentioned next and together with the unusual construction ('seven spirits who are before his throne'), some commentators think this is a reference to angels or archangels rather than the Holy Spirit. But the symbolic use of seven throughout the apocalypse (seven lamps, seven churches, seven seals, seven trumpets, seven bowls) suggests a reference to the Spirit in all its fullness. It occurs again in Revelation 3.1 ('These are the words of him who has the seven spirits'), Revelation 4.5 ('in front of the throne burn seven flaming torches, which are the seven spirits of God') and Revelation 5.6, where the Lamb (Christ) is said to have 'seven eyes, which are the seven spirits of God sent out into all the earth'. This last reference is an allusion to Zechariah 4.10 ('These seven are the eyes of the LORD, which range through the whole earth'), a chapter that has had a significant influence on John.

113

It begins with a reference to seven lamps (Zech. 4.2), which John identifies as the seven churches (Rev. 1.20). It then speaks of two olive trees (Zech. 4.3), which John will use in Revelation 11 for the two witnesses of the Church. Just before the reference to the seven spirits, the message to Zerubbabel is: 'Not by might, nor by power, *but by my spirit*' (Zech. 4.6), which strongly suggests that John's reference to the 'seven spirits' is a reference to the Holy Spirit.[4]

The description of Christ as 'the firstborn of the dead, and the ruler of the kings of the earth' is almost certainly an allusion to Psalm 89.27, where God says of David: 'I will make him the firstborn, the highest of the kings of the earth'. The change from 'firstborn' to 'firstborn of the dead' is clearly deliberate and George Caird was of the view that it represents John's *reinterpretation* of messianic rule. The psalm is not being 'applied' to Christ because of its honorific titles but in order to signal a 'profoundly Christian' reinterpretation. Christ's rule is *not* like the messianic rule of the psalm but comes through suffering and death, and he emerges as the firstborn of the dead. As we will see later, this coincides with Caird's view that all of the 'conquest' language in Revelation is to be reinterpreted because the 'gospel recognizes no other way of achieving these ends than the way of the Cross'.[5] Other commentators think this is too one-sided, noting that John is quite happy to include the title, 'highest of the kings of the earth', and indeed change it to 'ruler of the kings of the earth'.

The title 'faithful witness' could come from Proverbs 14.5 ('A faithful witness does not lie') or possibly Isaiah 55.4, where David is described as a 'witness to the peoples', but since 'firstborn' and 'ruler of kings' both come from Psalm 89.27, it is likely that John has Psalm 89.37 in mind. David is told that his line will continue for ever, which is then compared with the moon, a 'faithful witness' in the skies. Comparing Christ with the moon might seem an unlikely comparison but when all three phrases are taken together, it is clear that Psalm 89 was an important influence on John. There are no explicit quotations of Psalm 89 in the New Testament but according to the list of 'allusions and parallels' in UBS, it occurs several times in John's Gospel, as well as Luke, Paul and 1 Peter.[6] There is also some evidence (*Midrash Rabba Exod.* 19.7) that the rabbis understood Psalm 89 as a messianic text.

After the greetings, John records an oracle: 'Look! He is coming with the clouds; every eye will see him, even those who pierced him; and on his account all the tribes of the earth will wail' (Rev. 1.7). The first phrase is from Daniel 7.13 ('As I watched in the night visions, I saw one like a human being *coming with the clouds* of heaven') and occurs in Jesus' eschatological discourse (Mark 13.26) and trial before the High Priest (Mark 14.62). Of particular interest is that in Matthew's version of the eschatological discourse, the 'coming with the clouds' saying is preceded by the words: 'Then the sign of the Son of Man will appear in heaven, and then *all the tribes of the earth will mourn*' (Matt. 24.30). On its own, it is not clear where this phrase comes from but John's reference to 'those who pierced him' confirms that he has Zechariah 12.10 in mind ('And I will pour out a spirit of compassion and supplication on the house of David and the inhabitants of Jerusalem, so that, *when they look on the one whom they have pierced, they shall mourn for him*'). It is a fairly free allusion, with 'every eye will see' instead of 'when they look' and 'all the tribes of the earth will wail' (perhaps from Gen. 12.3) instead of 'they shall mourn' (referring to Israel). This makes it particularly difficult to decide whether the mourning/wailing represents remorse, as it does in Zechariah ('mourn *for him*'), or fear of judgement. Grant Osborne suggests that the ambiguity is deliberate, both themes (conversion and judgement) running through the rest of the book.[7]

The introduction ends with an affirmation: '"I am the Alpha and the Omega", says the Lord God, who is and who was and who is to come, the Almighty' (Rev. 1.8). Alpha and Omega are the first and last letters of the Greek alphabet and form what is known as a *merism*, where everything in between is included. In Jewish circles, the phrase was '*Aleph* to *Tau*', and the affirmation in Isaiah 44.6 ('I am the first and I am the last; besides me there is no god') is probably related. Thus in Revelation 21.6, the formula is expanded to 'I am the Alpha and the Omega, the beginning and the end', while in Revelation 22.13, it is the triple form: 'I am the Alpha and the Omega, the first and the last, the beginning and the end' (Rev. 22.13).

The inaugural vision (Revelation 1.12–18)

The resurrection narratives in the Gospels portray Jesus as one who can appear and disappear at will but his general appearance is not spectacular. Earlier in the Gospels, there is an account of a 'transfiguration', where his clothes became dazzling white (Mark 9.3) and according to Luke 9.29, his face was changed, though he does not say how. We might also mention Paul's experience on the way to Damascus where a 'light from heaven flashed around him' (Acts 9.3) and then he heard Jesus speak. But nothing compares with John's description of the risen Christ in Revelation 1:

> Then I turned to see whose voice it was that spoke to me, and on turning I saw seven golden lampstands, and in the midst of the lampstands I saw one like the Son of Man, clothed with a long robe and with a golden sash across his chest. His head and his hair were white as white wool, white as snow; his eyes were like a flame of fire, his feet were like burnished bronze, refined as in a furnace, and his voice was like the sound of many waters. In his right hand he held seven stars, and from his mouth came a sharp, two-edged sword, and his face was like the sun shining with full force. When I saw him, I fell at his feet as though dead. But he placed his right hand on me, saying, 'Do not be afraid; I am the first and the last, and the living one. I was dead, and see, I am alive for ever and ever; and I have the keys of Death and of Hades.'
> (Revelation 1.12–18)

The spoken words at the end ('first and last, and the living one') suggest that John is identifying Jesus with God (or an aspect of God) and this is reinforced by his description of the figure's head and hair being 'like white wool, white as snow'. This is almost certainly an allusion to Daniel 7.9, where the one who sits on the throne (whom Daniel calls 'Ancient of Days') has clothes that are 'white as snow' and whose hair is like 'pure wool'. However, the greater part of the inaugural vision identifies Jesus with the angel who explains the visions to Daniel:

> I looked up and saw a man *clothed in linen*, with a *belt of gold* from Uphaz around his waist. His body was like beryl, his face like lightning, *his eyes like flaming torches*, his arms and *legs like the gleam of burnished bronze*, and the *sound of his words like* the roar of a multitude ... and when I heard the sound of his words, *I fell* into a trance, face *to the ground. But then a hand touched me* and roused me to my hands and knees ... He said to me, 'Do not fear, Daniel.'   (Daniel 10.5–6, 9–10, 12)

When we also note that John seems to have gone out of his way to add details from other passages – the 'sound of many waters' echoes the noise of the creatures' wings in Ezekiel 1.24 and the 'sharp sword' echoes the servant's speech in Isaiah 49.2 – it is clearly more complicated than simply identifying Jesus with God. Jesus seems to bear the characteristics of many Old Testament figures and there are at least three ways of explaining this. The first is that John is simply aiming at rhetorical effect and is not trying to communicate specific theological themes from each passage. As George Caird says, 'John uses his allusions not as a code in which each symbol requires separate and exact translation, but rather for their evocative and emotive power.'[8]

Second, figures in the Old Testament who come from God (angels or messengers) or have been in God's presence (Moses), as well as objects such as God's throne, are often described in exalted language. Thus Moses' face glows when he speaks to

God (Exod. 34.35) and the description of the angel in Daniel 10.5–6 (lightning, flames of fire) is similar to the description of the throne in Daniel 7.9–10. Thus John is not so much identifying Jesus with particular figures (Daniel's angel, Isaiah's servant, Ezekiel's creatures) but demonstrating how he exhibits the Old Testament signs of 'proximity to God'.[9]

Third, although such visionary descriptions are largely absent from the New Testament, they do appear in other apocalyptic works. Thus in the *Apocalypse of Abraham*, the angel Yahoel has a body like sapphire, a face like chrysolite and hair like snow (11.1–3). In a fictional romance called *Joseph and Aseneth*, Aseneth sees a figure who looks like Joseph but 'his face was like lightning, and his eyes were like sunlight, and the hairs of his head like a flame of fire, and his hands and his feet like iron from the fire' (14.9). After reviewing a number of such works, Peter Carrell concludes that there was a common stock of imagery (snow, fire, sun, molten metals) that could be applied to a variety of exalted figures, as well as to God.[10] Indeed John can also apply such language to an angel: 'And I saw another mighty angel coming down from heaven, wrapped in a cloud, with a rainbow over his head; his face was like the sun, and his legs like pillars of fire' (Rev. 10.1–2). It is for this reason that scholars are divided as to whether the figure sitting on a cloud in Revelation 14 is Jesus or an angel, despite being described as 'one like the Son of Man' (Rev. 14.14).[11]

The throne vision (Revelation 4—5)

John's description of the throne and its attendants owes much to Ezekiel 1 and Isaiah 6. Thus the throne is surrounded by a 'rainbow that looks like an emerald' (Rev. 4.3/Ezek. 1.26, 28) and a 'sea of glass, like crystal' (Rev. 4.6/Ezek. 1.22), while from it come 'flashes of lightning, and rumblings . . . of thunder' (Rev. 4.5/Ezek. 1.4, 13) Four creatures are in attendance, with faces like a lion, an ox, a human and an eagle (Rev. 4.7/Ezek. 1.10, though each of Ezekiel's creatures has four faces) and are 'full of eyes all around and inside' (Rev. 4.8). This odd detail comes from Ezekiel 1.18, where the rims of the throne chariot were 'full of eyes all round'. It shows that John was not just copying Ezekiel's vision but transforming it. This is also seen in John's description of the creatures as having six wings instead of four and singing, 'Holy, holy, holy, the Lord God the Almighty, who was and is and is to come', a clear reference to the seraphim in Isaiah's vision (Isa. 6.2–3).

Like Ezekiel and Isaiah, John is extremely reserved in describing the actual appearance of God. Ezekiel says the figure on the throne seemed to have human shape but his only description is that the top half was like 'gleaming amber' and the bottom half like 'fire' (Ezek. 1.26–27). Isaiah simply says that he 'saw the Lord sitting on a throne, high and lofty; and the hem of his robe filled the temple' (Isa. 6.1). John offers a succinct comparison: 'And the one seated there looks like jasper and cornelian' (Rev. 4.3). There is considerable difficulty identifying the precious stones of the ancient world with their modern equivalents and the New Jerusalem Bible renders the two Greek words (*iaspis, sardion*) as 'diamond and ruby', assuming that John is referring to the purest white (whereas modern jasper comes in a number of colours) and a fiery red. Both stones are part of the priestly breastplate (Exod. 28.17–18) and the mythic description of the king of Tyre (Ezek. 28.13) but they do not figure in any of the Old Testament descriptions of God. Robert Thomas[12] thinks John's choice is symbolic, jasper/diamond standing for majesty or holiness and cornelian/ruby for judgement but it is hard to see how John's readers could have discerned this. What can be said is that both stones are prominent in the description of the New Jerusalem (Rev. 21.11, 18–20) and Grant Osborne[13] is probably correct that John's point is similar to 1 Timothy 6.16 ('It is he alone who has immortality and dwells in unapproachable light'), though it is unclear if John would have agreed with the next clause ('whom no one has ever seen or can see').

As well as the four creatures that surround the throne, there are 24 elders – probably representing the 12 tribes of Israel and the 12 apostles – who sing: 'You are worthy, our Lord and God, to receive glory and honour and power, for you created all things, and by your will they existed and were created' (Rev. 4.11). The thought is repeated in Revelation 10.5–6, where an angel swears 'by him who lives for ever and ever, who created heaven and what is in it, the earth and what is in it, and the sea and what is in it', and Revelation 14.6–7, where another angel exhorts every 'nation and tribe and language and people' to 'worship him who made heaven and earth, the sea and the springs of water'. That God is to be worshipped as Creator is frequent in the Psalms (8.3; 33.6–9; 95.1–5; 102.25; 136.1–9) and the formula 'as I live' is frequent in the prophets (Isa. 49.18; Jer. 22.24; Ezek. 5.11). But the particular phrase, 'by him who lives for ever and ever' points to Daniel 12.7, since the context is also of an angel raising his hand and swearing an oath. Here, God is revealed as the one who controls history and the period of struggle ('a time, two times, and half a time', i.e. three and a half years) is picked up by John in Revelation 13.5 as the 42 months that the beast will be allowed to exercise its authority.

If there are doubts as to whether the inaugural vision conveys specific theological meaning, most scholars regard Revelation 5.5–6 as one of the most important passages in the book. Continuing on from the throne vision of Revelation 4, John sees a scroll in God's right hand that only Jesus can open. When he does, a series of disasters are unleashed but it is the way that he is introduced that has attracted attention:

> Then one of the elders said to me, 'Do not weep. See, the Lion of the tribe of Judah, the Root of David, has conquered, so that he can open the scroll and its seven seals.' Then I saw between the throne and the four living creatures and among the elders a Lamb standing as if it had been slaughtered, having seven horns and seven eyes, which are the seven spirits of God sent out into all the earth. (Revelation 5.5–6)

The first affirmation alludes to the messianic hopes of Israel, particularly the prophetic promise to Judah in Genesis 49.9–10, and the 'root of Jesse' (David's father) in Isaiah 11.1, 10. This is what John heard. However, what he sees is a slaughtered lamb with seven horns and seven eyes. Josephine Massyngberde Ford thinks this is an image of power, citing *Testament of Joseph* 19.8, where a virgin from the tribe of Judah gives birth to a lamb which conquers its enemies, trampling them under foot. All would agree that 'seven horns' is a symbol of strength and texts like Revelation 17.14 ('they will make war on the Lamb, and the Lamb will conquer them, for he is Lord of lords and King of kings') make it clear that John's lamb is not weak and vulnerable but all-powerful, like a lion.[14]

On the other hand, most scholars think that John is intending a contrast: John *hears* about a lion but *sees* a slaughtered lamb. In other words, the messianic hopes of Israel are to be realized through the sacrificial death of Christ. Whether John is thinking of the Passover lamb, sacrificial lambs in general or the lamb of Isaiah 53.7 is difficult to determine but he is definitely not thinking of the conquering lamb of *Testament of Joseph* 19.8, a text which probably post-dates Revelation in any case.[15] Christ's victory was not by military might but voluntary self-sacrifice, as the hymn that follows makes clear:

> You are worthy to take the scroll and to open its seals, *for you were slaughtered and by your blood* you ransomed for God saints from every tribe and language and people and nation; you have made them to be a kingdom and priests serving our God, and they will reign on earth.   (Revelation 5.9–10)

However, the reason that Revelation 5.5–6 has been accorded such importance is not so much for its gospel message but the possibility that John has placed it here in order to act as an interpretative key for the rest of the book. Thus it can be shown that John frequently juxtaposes what he *sees* with what he *hears*. In the opening vision, John *sees* seven lampstands (Rev. 1.12)

121

and then *hears* that they are seven churches (Rev. 1.20). In Revelation 7, the order is reversed: John *hears* that 144,000 have been sealed (Rev. 7.4–8) and *sees* a 'great multitude that no one could count, from every nation, from all tribes and peoples and languages' (Rev. 7.9). The implication is that the 144,000 is not to be taken literally; it is a symbolic number (12×12×1,000) which is then explained as a countless multitude. In Revelation 12, John *sees* a heavenly battle between Michael and Satan but does not understand its meaning until he *hears* the heavenly voice. In Revelation 15, John *sees* those who have conquered the beast and *hears* the song of Moses and the Lamb. In Revelation 21, John *sees* a new heaven and earth and *hears* that God will wipe away every tear and make his dwelling with humanity. John clearly intends what he *sees* and what he *hears* to mutually interpret one another.

As a result, most scholars think that in Revelation 5.5–6, 'John overturns conventional expectations that the Messiah will subjugate Israel's enemies by conquest and might, and replaces that expectation with a new definition of conquest and might – a slaughtered Lamb.'[16] Thus when we read in the following chapter that the world's population seeks to hide from the 'wrath of the Lamb' (Rev. 6.16), Mark Bredin comments:

> The juxtaposition of 'Lamb' and 'wrath' may, at first sight, appear incomprehensible, as was the combination of Lion and Lamb in Revelation 5.5–6. John reinterprets 'wrath' by placing it alongside the most non-militaristic image, Lamb. Wrath no longer depicts a military, conquering God on the battlefield; God is not one who slays with a sword. Suffering love is the essence of wrath, and therefore suffering love is that which brings about God's judgement and kingdom.[17]

This is clearly an attractive interpretation for anyone who finds it difficult to reconcile the Jesus of the Gospels with the warlike figure of Revelation. But is it a case of wishful thinking? Could not the principle of juxtaposing what he *sees* with what he *hears* work the other way around? John introduces the lion, an obvious symbol of power and victory, in order to reinterpret the traditional Christian image of Christ as lamb. John's hearers know that Christ died for their sins (Rev. 1.5; 5.9); what John wishes to tell them is that he is also the powerful conqueror who will defeat their enemies and win the final victory:

> Then I saw heaven opened, and there was a white horse! Its rider is called Faithful and True, and *in righteousness he judges and makes war*. His eyes are like a flame of fire, and on his head are many diadems; and he has a name inscribed that no one knows but himself. *He is clothed in a robe dipped in blood*, and his name is called The Word of God. And the *armies of heaven*, wearing fine linen, white and pure, were following him on white horses. *From his mouth comes a sharp sword with which to strike down the nations, and he will rule them with a rod of iron; he will tread the wine press of the fury of the wrath of God the Almighty.* On his robe and on his thigh he has a name inscribed, *'King of kings and Lord of lords'*. (Revelation 19.11–16)

No one could miss the military imagery (war, blood, armies, sword, strike down) in this episode, much of it based on the Old Testament. In the inaugural vision, there was an allusion to Isaiah 49.2 ('from his mouth came a sharp, two-edged sword'). This is now combined with Isaiah 11.4 to state that the sword which comes from his mouth is 'to strike down the nations', which is then combined with Psalm 2.9, that he will 'rule them with a rod of iron'. Indeed, what he omits from Isaiah 11.4 is as interesting as what he borrows: 'with righteousness he shall judge the poor, and decide with equity for the meek of the earth; he shall strike the earth with the rod of his mouth.' The two positive statements (justice for the poor, equity for the meek) are omitted, leaving only the war imagery. In fact the verb 'to make war' (*polemeō*) occurs six times in Revelation and only once elsewhere in the New Testament (Jas. 4.2). It is used of Christ making war (Rev. 2.16; 19.11), angels making war (Rev. 12.7, twice) and people making war (Rev. 13.4; 17.14).

The war imagery continues with the reference to treading the wine press of God's wrath, which is probably an allusion to Isaiah 63.3 ('I have trodden the wine press alone ... I trod them in my anger and trampled them in my wrath'). This would also explain the reference to Christ's robe being dipped in blood since Isaiah continues, 'their juice spattered on my garments, and stained all my robes'. The image of treading the wine press of God's wrath has already occurred in Revelation 14, where the coming judgement is likened to a harvesting of the earth:

> So the angel swung his sickle over the earth and gathered the vintage of the earth, and he threw it into the great wine press of the wrath of God. And the wine press was trodden outside the city, and blood flowed from the wine press, as high as a horse's bridle, for a distance of about two hundred miles.
>
> (Revelation 14.19–20)

As for the phrase, 'King of kings and Lord of lords', the precise form does not occur in the Hebrew Bible, though Deuteronomy 10.17 speaks of 'God of gods and Lord of lords' and Daniel 2.47 has 'God of gods and Lord of kings'. It does occur in one of the LXX's additions to Daniel (4.37) but perhaps we need not look for a precise source. John is asserting that Christ is the ultimate power, the power associated with God alone in the Old Testament, and so the outcome of the battle is not in doubt. The beast and the false prophet are captured and thrown into the lake of fire (Rev. 19.20) and 'the rest were killed by the sword of the rider on the horse, the sword that came from his mouth; and all the birds were gorged with their flesh' (Rev. 19.21). Here, John draws on the imagery of Ezekiel 39.17–20 where Gog and his armies are defeated and the birds invited to feed on their flesh. We seem to be as far from a sacrificial lamb as it is possible to imagine.

Or are we? Caird points out that the blood on Christ's robe cannot be the blood of his enemies as the battle has not yet been fought. It must be the blood of the martyrs: 'The Rider bears on his garment the indelible traces of the death of his followers, just as he bears on his body the indelible marks of his own passion.'[18] One might counter this by saying that although the battle of Revelation 19.20 has not been fought, we have already had the great harvest of Revelation 14 with its 200 miles of blood; no wonder Christ's robe is soaked in it! However, Caird does not think that the harvest is referring to the destruction of God's enemies, as it is in the Old Testament. Rather, it refers to the Jesus tradition concerning the ingathering of the elect (Mark 13.27; 1 Thess. 4.15–17). He notes that Revelation 13 ended with the threat of death for Christ's followers and Revelation 15 begins with a vision of the martyrs' victory song in heaven. Thus it is likely that the intervening chapter deals with their death. In a reversal of Old Testament imagery, the harvest is not the death of God's enemies but the death of his followers and so it is the shedding of their own blood that constitutes the victory, as it was with Christ.

It should also be noted that the sword that comes from Christ's mouth is not a real sword but refers to the 'piercing' nature of his speech, as in Hebrews 4.12: 'Indeed, the word of God is living and active, sharper than any two-edged sword, piercing until it divides soul from spirit, joints from marrow; it is able to judge the thoughts and intentions of the heart.' So if the sword is metaphorical, then it is likely that the war is metaphorical, despite the graphic language that is used. Bauckham summarizes: 'In the eschatological destruction of evil in Revelation there is no place for real armed violence, but there is ample space of [*sic*] the imagery of armed violence.'[19] If this is correct, then John has drawn much of his violent imagery from the Old Testament in order to subvert it. He offers a Christian reinterpretation where the only way to victory is through voluntary self-sacrifice.

Dragon, beast and false prophet

Although Genesis 3 lays the blame for the first temptation on the serpent, there is very little in the rest of the Old Testament to suggest that human sin is incited by external forces. The book of Job has a mysterious account where 'the accuser' (Heb: 'the satan'; Greek: 'the devil') challenges God with the proposition that the only reason Job is faithful is because God looks after him; take that away and Job would soon curse God. But there is nothing in the book to suggest that 'the satan' directly interferes in human affairs. The only other passage of note is Daniel 10, where the angel tells Daniel that he was delayed because the prince of Persia opposed him for 21 days until Michael came to his aid (Dan. 10.13). The passage suggests that some sort of angelic war is going on but is otherwise unexplained. However, by the time we get to the New Testament period there is a considerable literature on the influence of angels and demons on human affairs. Indeed, in the Gospels, the devil or Satan is seen as the force behind temptation (Matt. 4.1–11), demon possession (Mark 3.20–30), certain types of illness (Luke 13.16), unbelief (Luke 8.12) and betrayal (John 13.2). But the book of Revelation is the first to connect this explicitly with the serpent of Genesis:

> And war broke out in heaven; Michael and his angels fought against the dragon. The dragon and his angels fought back, but they were defeated, and there was no longer any place for them in heaven. The great dragon was thrown down, that ancient serpent, who is called the Devil and Satan, the deceiver of the whole world – he was thrown down to the earth, and his angels were thrown down with him.   (Revelation 12.7–9)

There are two main interpretations of this difficult text. The first was popularized in Milton's *Paradise Lost* and suggests that John is offering an explanation for the presence of evil in the garden of Eden. Prior to creation, there was a 'fall from heaven' and this is alluded to in texts like Isaiah 14.12 ('How you are fallen from heaven, O Day Star, son of Dawn!') and Ezekiel 28.16 ('you were filled with violence, and you sinned; so I cast you as a profane thing from the mountain of God'). Historically, these texts are referring to the kings of Babylon and Tyre respectively, but the extreme language could suggest that they are modelled on a far greater 'fall from grace'. A primordial battle is alluded to in Psalm 74.14 ('You crushed the heads of Leviathan') and Isaiah 27.1 identifies Leviathan with the 'twisting serpent'. Grant Osborne is a modern advocate of this position, citing these texts, Jesus' words in Luke 10.18 ('I watched Satan fall from heaven like a flash of lightning') and the fact that the theme is found in other apocalyptic documents (*1 Enoch* 1—6; *2 Enoch* 29.4–5 (J); *Sibylline Oracles* 5.528–9; *Life of Adam and Eve* 13.1–2). On this view, John is not only offering an explanation of the serpent in the garden of Eden but of the presence of evil throughout world history.

On the other hand, the dragon's fall appears to be the result of Christ's victory (Rev. 12.5–6) and its purpose in the narrative is to explain the persecution of the Church. This is stated first by saying that the dragon goes in pursuit of the 'woman who had given birth to the male child' (Rev. 12.13) and then that it 'went off to make war on the rest of her children, those who keep the commandments of God and hold the testimony of Jesus' (Rev. 12.17). This latter phrase is almost certainly a reference to the Church at large and not simply to Jesus' siblings. Consequently, many scholars think that the woman is not specifically Mary but the 'messianic community' that gave birth to Jesus.[20] Be that as it may, the point is that it is Jesus' victory on the cross that triggers the defeat of the dragon and thus in this interpretation, John's reference to the serpent is simply to assert its defeat.

The dragon's strategy is to enlist two beasts, one from the sea (Rev. 13.1–10) and one from the earth (Rev. 13.11–18), to attack God's people. The first beast is modelled on Daniel's vision of four beasts emerging from the sea (Dan. 7.1–8), which represented a succession of empires (Dan. 7.17), generally thought to be Babylonian, Medo-Persian, Greek and Roman. What is of note is that whereas Daniel has four beasts/empires, John has combined them into one beast/empire that not only blasphemes God (Rev. 13.6/Dan. 7.19) but is 'allowed to make war on the saints and to conquer them' (Rev. 13.7). The second beast 'makes the earth and its inhabitants worship the first beast' (Rev. 13.12) by performing signs and wonders. It is called the 'false prophet' in Revelation 19.20, where it is consigned to the lake of fire, along with the first beast. Most scholars believe that John is deliberately constructing an evil trinity (dragon, beast, false prophet), especially as one of the heads of the beast from the sea is said to have received a 'death-blow, but its mortal wound had been healed' (Rev. 13.3), a parody of Christ's death and resurrection. The beast from the earth or false prophet is also referred to by the cryptic number 666, which may have referred to a specific individual in the first century (Nero, Caligula) but which, since the interpretation has been lost, has been applied to numerous individuals down the ages. The practice of representing words by numbers is known as *gematria* and is based on the principle that letters can also have a numerical value. Thus the Greek letters of Jesus (*Iēsous*) add up to 888 and it is possible that 666 is related to this (imperfection personified) and was never intended to point to a specific individual.[21]

Judgements and disasters

The climax of the book of Revelation is the defeat of these evil powers but, prior to this, John narrates a series of earthly disasters, drawing on a range of sources. They are arranged in three sets of seven, known as the seals, the trumpets and the bowls. The pattern is complicated by the fact that the seventh seal leads into the seven trumpets and the seventh trumpet leads into the seven bowls. The nature of the calamity is summarized in Table 5.1.

Table 5.1

	Seven seals (6.1–17; 8.1–2)	Seven trumpets (8.6—9.21; 11.15–19)	Seven bowls (16.1–21)
1	White horse – conquest.	*Hail* and fire mixed with blood. One third of earth burned up.	*Foul and painful sores* on those with mark of beast.
2	Red horse – incites warfare.	*Sea turned to blood.* One third of all sea creatures killed.	*Sea to blood* – everything died.
3	Black horse – famine.	*Rivers turned to blood.* Many died.	*Rivers to blood* – angel responds that it is just.
4	Pale green horse – sword, famine, *pestilence*, animals.	One third of sun, stars and moon darkened.	Sun allowed to scorch people – but they did not repent.
5	Martyrs cry out for vengeance.	*Locusts* torture those without the seal for five months.	*Darkness covers the earth* – but they did not repent.
6	Earthquake, sun blackened, moon turned to blood, stars fall.	Cavalry of 200 million kill one third of humankind.	*Foul spirits like frogs* – ready for Armageddon.
7	Silence in heaven.	Kingdom of God announced.	Earthquake and *hail* – people cursed God.

One source for these descriptions is the plagues inflicted on Pharaoh and Egypt in order to deliver Israel from slavery (Exod. 7.17—12.32). The 10 plagues consisted of (1) *rivers into blood* (2) *frogs* (3) gnats (4) flies (5) *pestilence* (6) *boils* (7) *hail* (8) *locusts* (9) *darkness* (10) death of first-born. This appears to be the basis for the bowls (see italics), especially with the repeated refrain that despite these calamities, the people still did not

Table 5.2

Matthew 24.29	*Revelation 6.12–14*	*Revelation 8.12*
Immediately after the suffering of those days the *sun will be darkened*, and the	When he opened the sixth seal, I looked, and there came a great earthquake; *the sun became black* as sackcloth,	The fourth angel blew his trumpet, and a third of the *sun* was struck,
moon will not give its light; the *stars will fall* from heaven,	the full *moon became like blood*, and the *stars of the sky fell* to the earth as the fig tree drops its winter fruit when shaken by a gale.	and a third of the *moon*, and a third of the *stars*, so that a third of their light was darkened; a third of the day was kept from shining, and
and the powers of heaven will be shaken.	The sky vanished like a scroll rolling itself up, and every mountain and island was removed from its place.	likewise the night.

repent (cf. Exod. 7.22; 8.15, 19, 31 etc.). The cosmic signs in sun, moon and stars draws on such passages as Isaiah 13.10 (they no longer give their light), Isaiah 34.4 (stars fall like figs from a tree, sky rolled up like a scroll), Joel 2.10 (the earth quakes) and Joel 2.31 (moon turns to blood). These passages also lie behind Jesus' eschatological discourse and it is possible that this is the inspiration behind John's vision (see Table 5.2). If so, then it would appear that he has gone behind that tradition and taken further details from the passages listed above.

The first four seals unleash four coloured horses (white, red, black, pale green) and this is probably inspired by the four horses of Zechariah 1.7–11 (red, red, sorrel, white) and 6.1–8 (red, black, white, dappled grey). In Zechariah the horses patrol the earth, but in Revelation they bring a sequence of disasters which, unlike the Egyptian plagues, are largely the consequences of human sin (conquest, warfare, famine, sword). It is a little confusing that John will later describe Christ as sitting on a white horse (Rev. 19.11) and some have suggested that it should therefore be given a positive meaning here, such as the triumph of the gospel. However, in view of the Zechariah parallel, it is more likely that the four horses should be taken together and represent a progression from conquest and civil war to pestilence and death.

Witness and struggle

The seven messages to the churches offer a glimpse of the struggles faced by the churches. There are internal problems, as with those who advocate eating idol meat, an issue faced by Paul in Corinth. John uses several Old Testament characters to describe/demonize them. They are like Balaam who 'taught Balak to put a stumbling-block before the people of Israel, so that they would eat food sacrificed to idols and practise fornication' (Rev. 2.14). This is not what the Old Testament says and like Jude and 2 Peter, John is possibly drawing on apocryphal traditions. Their leader appears to be a certain Jezebel 'who calls herself a prophet and is teaching and beguiling my servants to practise fornication and to eat food sacrificed to idols' (Rev. 2.20). It is possible that this was her name – and John would have thought it apt – but it is probably a name that John gives her in order to associate her behaviour with the biblical Jezebel who sought to kill Elijah (1 Kings 18—21). There is also opposition from those that John describes as the 'synagogue of Satan' (Rev. 3.9). It is unclear if this refers to Jews in general or specifically those who are persecuting the Church. His promise that one day they will come and bow down before their feet appears to be a deliberate reversal of the promise of Isaiah that in the last days, the nations will come and bow down before the Jews (Isa. 60.14).

In Revelation 11, the witness of the Church is described using Zechariah's symbol of the two olive trees. For a period, their witness is irresistible and like Elijah, they have 'authority to shut the sky, so that no rain may fall during the days of their prophesying', and like Moses, they have 'authority over the waters to turn them into blood, and to strike the earth with every kind of plague, as often as they desire' (Rev. 11.6). However, they are then killed by the beast and 'their dead bodies will lie in the street of the great city that is prophetically called Sodom and Egypt, where also their Lord was crucified' (Rev. 11.8). If this is intended as a geographical reference, then it must be Jerusalem, but it is probably symbolic: they will die as Christ died. But just as Christ was raised from the dead, so after three and a half days, 'the breath of life from God entered them, and they stood on their feet, and those who saw them were terrified' (Rev. 11.11). This is an allusion to Ezekiel 37.10 where he predicts the restoration of Israel under the image of dry bones coming back to life: 'I prophesied as he commanded me, and the *breath came into them, and they lived, and stood on their feet*, a vast multitude.' The parallel is that in both passages, God's people (or their representatives) are brought back to life by the breath/spirit of God, though in other ways, the passages are very different.

If the dragon, beast and false prophet are the evil trinity opposed to God, they are represented on earth by a prostitute 'drunk with the blood of the saints and the blood of the witnesses to Jesus' (17.6). This offensive image changes to a city in Revelation 18, sucking the life out of its inhabitants in order to satisfy the extravagant lifestyle of its rulers. John draws on a range of passages to describe this but Ezekiel's lament against Tyre is the main inspiration. Both passages include a list of luxurious imports, including a reference to slaves (Rev. 18.13/Ezek. 27.13), while describing the effect of the city's destruction in the terms shown in Table 5.3 (interestingly occurring in reverse order in Revelation):

Table 5.3

Ezekiel	Revelation
I will silence the music of your songs; the sound of your lyres shall be heard no more. (26.13)	the sound of harpists and minstrels and of flautists and trumpeters will be heard in you no more. (18.22)
They throw dust on their heads and wallow in ashes. (27.30)	And they threw dust on their heads, as they wept and mourned. (18.19)
In their wailing they raise a lamentation for you, and lament over you: 'Who was ever destroyed like Tyre in the midst of the sea?' (27.32)	And all shipmasters and seafarers, sailors and all whose trade is on the sea, stood far off and cried out as they saw the smoke of her burning, 'What city was like the great city?' (18.17–18)
The merchants among the peoples hiss at you; you have come to a dreadful end and shall be no more for ever. (27.36)	And the merchants of the earth weep and mourn for her, since no one buys their cargo any more. (18.11)

Final salvation

Despite the sheer quantity of judgement oracles (or perhaps because of it), the book is punctuated by visions of salvation which reach their conclusion in Revelation 20—22. This begins in the seven messages to the churches, where each church is given a particular promise:

Ephesus   – eat from the tree of life in the Paradise of God
Smyrna   – avoid the second death
Pergamum   – partake of the hidden manna, receive a white stone
Thyatira   – rule the nations, receive the morning star
Sardis   – receive white robes, name not erased from book of life
Philadelphia   – made a pillar of the temple
Laodicea   – receive a place on the throne

What is interesting about these promises is that while they have some basis in the Old Testament (tree of life, rule the nations, book of life), they mainly draw on extra-biblical traditions. For example, the 'tree of life' barely gets a mention in the Old Testament[22] but in Jewish tradition (*1 Enoch* 24—25; *4 Ezra* 8; *Testament of Levi* 18), when Adam and Eve were ejected from the garden of Eden, the tree of life was transported to the eschatological paradise where the elect will one day feed on it.

The promise of the hidden manna appears to draw on traditions where prior to the destruction of the temple, Jeremiah (or an angel) was told to save the ark of the covenant, with its jar of manna (Exod. 16.32–34). This would then await the coming of the Messiah, who would return it to a restored temple (2 Macc. 2.4–7; *2 Baruch* 6.7–10). It thus becomes part of the 'messianic feast' tradition. Similarly with the notion of the 'second death', which does not occur in the Old Testament but is found in a number of the Aramaic Targums (Deut. 33.6; Isa. 22.14; 65.6, 15; Jer. 51.39, 57). Thus the Hebrew of Deuteronomy 33.6 refers to the tribe of Reuben ('May Reuben live, and not die out, even though his numbers are few') but the Targum reads: 'Let Reuben live in eternal life and die not the second death.'

Before the opening of the seventh seal, John has a vision of 144,000 receiving a mark of protection on their foreheads (7.2–3). The number is symbolic since John goes on to say that he saw 'a great multitude that no one could count' (7.9). This is almost certainly based on Ezekiel 9.4 ('Go through the city, through Jerusalem, and put a mark on the foreheads of those who sigh and groan over all the abominations that are committed in it'), since both are followed by an account of an angel taking coals from the altar and hurling them over the earth (Rev. 8.5/Ezek. 10.2). However, the seal does not protect them from death for the interpreting angel tells John that they are those 'who have come out of the great ordeal; they have washed their robes and made them white in the blood of the Lamb'

Table 5.4

Isaiah 49.10; 25.8; Psalm 23.1–2	Revelation 7.16–17
[T]hey shall not *hunger* or *thirst*, neither *scorching* wind nor *sun* shall strike them down, for he who has pity on them will lead them,	They will *hunger* no more, and *thirst* no more; the *sun* will not strike them, nor any *scorching* heat; for the Lamb at the centre of the throne will be their *shepherd*, and he will
and by *springs of water* will *guide them* . . . Then the Lord GOD *will wipe away the tears* from all faces . . .	*guide them* to *springs of the water* of life, and *God will wipe away every tear* from their eyes.
The LORD is my *shepherd* . . . he leads me beside still *waters*.	

(Rev. 7.14). It is evidently the seal of the elect, perhaps a reference to their baptism (cf. 2 Cor. 1.22; Eph. 1.13), but not protection from death.

The moving pastoral image in Revelation 7.16–17 is almost a quotation from Isaiah 49.10, along with a phrase from Isaiah 25.8 and perhaps a reminiscence of Psalm 23.2. It affirms that life's struggles (hunger, thirst, scorching heat) will be no more, past pains will be forgotten (God will wipe away every tear) and a new environment awaits them (by springs of living water). The extent of John's dependence on the Old Testament can be seen in Table 5.4.

Before John begins three chapters of judgement in Revelation 16 (seven bowls), 17 (destruction of the harlot and the beast) and 18 (fall of Babylon), he narrates a vision of the saints in heaven who are singing 'the song of Moses, the servant of God, and the song of the Lamb' (Rev. 15.3). What is puzzling about the song that follows is that it bears no similarity to the song of Moses in Exodus 15 but is based on Psalm 86.8–10, supplemented by a number of texts which share common vocabulary (Deut. 32.4; Ps. 145.7; Jer. 10.6–7). Psalm 86 proclaims the incomparability of God ('There is none like you among the gods ... you alone are God'), the greatness of his works ('For you are great and do wondrous things') and the universality of his salvation ('All the nations you have made shall come and bow down before you, O Lord, and shall glorify your name'). Given the fact that 'the nations' have been the subject of judgement in Revelation 6—14, the inclusion of a hymn that proclaims their salvation can only be deliberate.

> Great and amazing are your deeds, Lord God the Almighty! Just and true are your ways, King of the nations! Lord, who will not fear and glorify your name? For you alone are holy. All nations will come and worship before you, for your judgements have been revealed.   .   (Revelation 15.3–4)

The millennium

Having disposed of the beast and false prophet in the lake of fire (Rev. 19.20), the dragon is locked away for 1,000 years (Rev. 20.3) and 'those who had been beheaded for their testimony' came to life and reigned with Christ. After the 1,000 years are up, the dragon is released and gathers the nations for one final battle but is immediately defeated and thrown into the lake of fire (Rev. 20.7–10), along with Death itself (Rev. 20.14). Books are opened and the dead are judged according to their deeds (Rev. 20.12). Then comes John's vision of a new heaven and earth (cf. Isa. 65.17), a suitable climax to the book (and perhaps the whole Bible), which picks up on earlier promises (no more tears, living water, tree of life) and focuses on a vision of the New Jerusalem.

Before we consider this, a word needs to be said about the millennial reign of the saints. Functionally, it is the fulfilment of earlier promises that those who overcome will reign with Christ (Rev. 2.26–27) but its interpretation has always been a matter of controversy. Some take it literally and believe that history will end with the saints ruling the earth, either before Christ's second coming (premillennial) or after it (postmillennial).

Others point out that if the phrase 'those who had been beheaded' is taken literally, the majority of saints down the ages would be excluded and we have already seen how numbers have symbolic meanings in Revelation. Thus a view popularized by Augustine is that the 1,000 years stands for the Church age (amillennial), where the saints have already come to life (spiritually) and reign with Christ until evil is finally defeated. There is no immediate Old Testament background for this but a messianic reign of various lengths is known in Jewish tradition.[23]

The New Jerusalem

In Revelation 21.9, John is told that he will see the 'bride, the wife of the Lamb' but what he sees is the 'holy city Jerusalem coming down out of heaven from God' (Rev. 21.10). His description owes much to Ezekiel's vision of a restored temple. For example, both prophets are transported by God to a high mountain (Rev. 21.10/Ezek. 40.2) and see a structure that radiates with the glory of God (Rev. 21.11/Ezek. 43.5). Both see an angel with a measuring rod (Rev. 21.15/Ezek. 40.3) and the various dimensions are given (many chapters in Ezekiel). Both cities have twelve gates, three on each side, which are said to represent the twelve tribes of Israel (Rev. 21.12–13/Ezek. 48.30–35). John adds that the wall has twelve foundations 'and on them the twelve names of the twelve apostles of the Lamb' (Rev. 21.14). This is one of the reasons why the 24 elders that surround the throne (Rev. 4.4, 10; 5.8; 11.16; 19.4) might represent the twelve tribes (Israel) and the twelve apostles (Church). However, it is John's description of the river that runs through the city and the miraculous tree of life that confirms that Ezekiel is his main source (see Table 5.5).

Ezekiel 47.12 is the only passage in the Old Testament that significantly draws on the 'tree of life' passage from Genesis and represents a significant development. Instead of a single tree in the garden, it is now 'all kinds of trees' and they grow on either side of a life-giving river (Ezek. 47.9). Their fruitfulness

Table 5.5

Ezekiel 47.12	Revelation 22.1–2
On the banks, on *both sides of the river*, there will grow all kinds of trees for food. Their leaves will not wither nor their fruit fail, but they will bear fresh *fruit every month*, because the *water* for them *flows from the* sanctuary. Their fruit will be for food, *and their leaves for healing.*	Then the angel showed me the *river* of the *water* of life, bright as crystal, *flowing from the* throne of God and of the Lamb through the middle of the street of the city. *On either side of the river is the tree* of life with its twelve kinds of *fruit*, producing its *fruit each month*; *and the leaves of the tree are for the healing* of the nations.

is demonstrated by bearing fruit every month rather than every year and a particular function is assigned to their leaves: they bring healing. John further specifies that the river flows from God's throne (and the Lamb) and the healing extends to the nations. Indeed, John will go on to describe the 'kings of the earth' bringing their glory into the city (Rev. 21.24). However, John does not follow Ezekiel in speaking of 'trees' in the plural, though some scholars believe that this is what John meant, since 'the tree' is said to be on either side of the river. Austin Farrer illustrated this by noting how an English-speaking person might say that a field was 'planted with oak'.[24] On the other hand, since John spoke of the singular 'tree of life' in the promise to Ephesus and does so again in Revelation 22.14 and 19, it may be that he wishes to maintain the allusion to Genesis, even though it has resulted in an impossible visual image.

Given that John is drawing on Ezekiel's vision of a restored temple, what stands out in John's description of the New Jerusalem is that it does not have a temple, for its temple 'is the Lord God the Almighty and the Lamb' (Rev. 21.22). There is debate as to whether Ezekiel envisaged an actual temple or is referring to an idealized eschatological temple. The long lists of precise dimensions suggest the former but the miraculous river and life-giving trees could suggest the latter. Either way, John is clearly making an important theological point; there will be no need for mediation in the New Jerusalem since God and the Lamb will be present to everybody. Thus the promise to Israel in Ezekiel 37.27 ('My dwelling-place shall be with them; and I will be their God, and they shall be my people') is expanded in Revelation 21.3 to include non-Israelites ('See, the home of God is among mortals. He will dwell with them; they will be his *peoples*,[25] and God himself will be with them'). When it is remembered that the promise to Ezekiel is itself a reaffirmation of the promise given to Abraham (Gen. 17.7–8), Moses (Exod. 29.45) and the prophets (Jer. 24.7; Zech. 8.8), John is offering a vision of 'paradise restored'. The original paradise envisaged God dwelling with Adam and Eve in the garden of Eden but that was disrupted by disobedience. That has now been overcome, evil and rebellion have been removed and God will once again dwell with humanity – not in a garden but in the New Jerusalem. The magnificence of this new abode is expressed in terms of a precious jewel ('It has the glory of God and a radiance like a very rare jewel, like jasper, clear as crystal' – Rev. 21.11), perfect measurements ('The city lies foursquare . . . its length and width and height are equal – Rev. 21.16) and radiant walls ('adorned with every jewel' – Rev. 21.19) and gates ('each of the gates is a single pearl' – Rev. 21.21). Although it was many centuries before the book of Revelation took its place as the last book of the Bible, it clearly intends to bring the biblical story to a conclusion.[26]

Conclusion

Two things stand out from this survey of John's allusions to Scripture. The first is that many of John's visions are either modelled on sections of Scripture (descriptions of God and Christ, throne room, heavenly worship, four horses, evil beasts, plagues, disasters, harvest of blood, messianic rule, tree of life,

New Jerusalem) or are composed in scriptural language ('breath of life entered them'; 'guide them to springs of water'). The implication would appear to be that John wished his readers to see his visions in continuity with Scripture, bringing to a conclusion the hopes and aspirations of its prophets and people. Richard Bauckham gives his collection of studies the title, *The Climax of Prophecy*, highlighting the fact that the majority of John's allusions come from the Prophets (and Psalms) rather than the Pentateuch.[27]

On the other hand, it is equally clear that John is highly selective in what he takes from the Old Testament and is not constrained either by the wording of the original or by its original meaning. Thus in his use of Psalm 89 in Revelation 1.5, 'firstborn' has become 'firstborn of the dead' and 'highest of the kings' has become 'ruler of the kings'. In the allusion to Zechariah 12.10 in Revelation 1.7, 'when they look' has become 'every eye will see' and 'they shall mourn' (referring to Israel) has become 'all the tribes of the earth will wail'. In terms of changes of meaning, Daniel sees four beasts emerging from the sea and is told that they represent a succession of evil empires. One might have thought that John would identify the current regime (Rome) with the fourth beast and show that its predicted downfall is imminent. In fact, John removes the idea of sequence and describes a single beast that incorporates elements from all four of Daniel's beasts. It is not necessarily an 'improper' use of Scripture but hardly what Daniel had in mind. The same can be said of Ezekiel's temple vision. The statement that the New Jerusalem does not have a temple because God and Christ are its temple might be a profound reinterpretation of Ezekiel but it is hardly what Ezekiel was thinking of when he spent chapter after chapter describing its various measurements.

In terms of a theory of composition, we might put it like this: Did John have a vision of the future (and present) and use Scripture to describe it (a rhetorical model), or did his vision come from Scripture, either by exegesis (a scribal model) or meditation (a mystical model)? Those who are most impressed by the similarities opt for a scribal/exegetical model, concluding that John's careful study of Scripture has enabled him to offer a theological synthesis which captures the true intent of the biblical authors. For example, Bauckham argues that the song to be sung in the new age (Rev. 15.3–4) is not simply an amalgam of worship texts but has been derived by careful exegesis of Exodus 15. Although there are no words in common, he argues that John was led by verbal association from Exodus 15.11 ('who is like you, O LORD, among the gods?') to three other texts (Ps. 86.8–10; 98.1–2; Jer. 10.7) where similar words occur. In this way, John was able to deduce the content of the new song. Greg Beale also thinks that John uses texts with their original context very much in mind.

On the other hand, those who are more struck by the differences between Revelation and Scripture opt for either a rhetorical or mystical model. The former begins with an analysis of John's rhetorical purposes and seeks to show how he uses Scripture to support his case. This applies both to his choice of Scripture – he only alludes to those texts that support the point he is trying to make – and what he does with them. Caird is a good example of this approach, where the fact of Christ's death and resurrection causes John to reinterpret the biblical texts. Thus the original meaning of Isaiah 63 is that God defeats his enemies and their blood has stained his garments. But John wishes to exclude such a meaning because he wants to show that Christian victory comes through voluntary self-sacrifice, not the death of one's enemies. Thus he reinterprets the 'blood' so that it now refers to the martyrs rather than God's enemies. Elisabeth Schüssler Fiorenza is also an advocate of a 'rhetorical' model, stating that John 'does not interpret the Old Testament but uses its words, images, phrases, and patterns as a language arsenal in order to make his own theological statement or express his own prophetic vision'.[28]

An important advocate of the 'mystical' model is Chris Rowland. He recognizes that a degree of planning has gone into the structure of the book and that John is certainly harnessing key images from the Scriptures to make his point. But Rowland wants to do justice to John's claim to be 'in the spirit' (Rev. 1.10; 4.2) and a receiver of visions. Texts and images have come together in John's mind but not through exegesis or attention to original context. They are more like dreams, which jump about without any apparent logic, and yet reveal some of our most basic hopes and fears. Thus before he comments on the text of Revelation, he invites us to contemplate some contemporary pictures to get us 'in the mood'. As with Revelation, modern art only 'works' if one has some familiarity with the images (like a political cartoon) but such 'contexts' do not determine their meaning. Indeed, Rowland questions whether 'authorial intention' is the appropriate goal for a work like Revelation. If asked why his use of the four horses differs from that found in Zechariah, John would most likely have replied, 'I was in the spirit.'[29]

Excursus: the Letters of John and Scripture

The documents traditionally known as the Letters of John consist of a homily of five chapters (1 John), where author and recipients are not named, followed by two short letters (13 and 15 verses respectively) from someone who calls himself 'The Elder', writing to 'the elect lady and her children' (2 John 1) and 'the beloved Gaius' (3 John 1). Church tradition associated this elder with John the apostle, thought to be the author of the Fourth Gospel and the book of Revelation. Scholars today are more inclined to think of a 'Johannine community' than common authorship, though the issue continues to be debated. There are no explicit quotations in the three works, though the advice not to emulate Cain in 1 John 3.12 is clearly a reference to Genesis 4.8. Otherwise, there are about 10 places where it has been argued that particular phrases may echo biblical language, but only in a few cases does this appear to be deliberate.

Cain and Abel

As we have seen, Hebrews 11.4 offers Abel as an example of faith and righteousness but 1 John 3.12 alludes to Cain as a warning: 'We must not be like Cain who was from the evil one and murdered his brother. And why did he murder him? Because his own deeds were evil and his brother's righteous.' Since Cain is not mentioned again in the Hebrew Bible and only once in the LXX (4 Macc. 18.11), the author is probably drawing on Jewish tradition. Thus in the *Apocalypse of Abraham* 24.5, Cain's actions are linked with the serpent/adversary of Genesis 3 and in the *Testament of Dan* 7.1–5, Cain's envy and hatred is linked to Beliar, an alternative name for the devil. The Genesis story focuses on Cain's choice but the author of 1 John considers choice to be an indicator of character and hence Cain is 'from the evil one'. Similarly, those who took the decision to leave the congregation – to set up rival congregations according to 2 and 3 John – show themselves to be 'antichrists' (1 John 2.18–28), even though they once belonged to the congregation.

Other allusions

The most convincing allusion occurs in 1 John 1.8–9, where a negative proposition ('If we say that we have no sin, we deceive ourselves') is followed by the positive ('If we confess our sins, he who is faithful and just will forgive us our sins and cleanse us from all unrighteousness'). Some of the language may be drawn from Deuteronomy 32.4 ('A *faithful* God, without deceit, *just* and upright is he') and David's confession in Psalm 32.5 ('I will confess my transgressions') but it is Proverbs 28.13 where we find both aspects: 'No one who conceals transgressions will prosper, but one who confesses and forsakes them will obtain mercy.' Given the nature of the book of Proverbs, it is unlikely that our author intends his readers to look up the passage. It is more that the pattern of negative followed by positive sounds 'biblical' and is therefore more convincing. We might say the same about the verse before (1 John 1.7) where 'walking in the light' and 'cleansing from sin' may allude to Proverbs 20.9 and Isaiah 2.5 respectively, but the effect is not dependent on knowing the particular passages.

The exhortation in 1 John 3.17 ('How does God's love abide in anyone who has the world's goods and sees a brother or sister in need and yet refuses help?') could easily stem from Christian tradition but some scholars see in it an allusion to Deuteronomy 15.7–8. The passage warns against being 'hard-hearted or 'tight-fisted' towards the 'needy neighbour' by reminding them that it was God who gave them the land in the first place. There is no parallel to God's love abiding in someone but the idea is similar.

Third, since Isaiah 53 was clearly used in the early Church to explain Christ's death, some have wondered if it lies in the background of the statement in 1 John 3.5: 'You know that he was revealed to take away sins, and in him there is no sin.' There is no single verse of Isaiah 53 that says both these things but verses 4 and 11 speak of bearing our sins and verse 9 suggests his innocence ('he had done no violence, and there was no deceit in his mouth').

Lastly, there are texts where a particular phrase can be paralleled in Scripture and is probably no more than the use of biblical language. Thus 1 John 2.10 affirms that for those who live in love, nothing will cause them to stumble (cf. Ps. 119.165). A few verses on, we read of sins forgiven 'on account of his name' (1 John 2.12); something similar is said in Psalm 25.11. The statement that God's commandments are not burdensome can be paralleled in Deuteronomy 30.11 ('Surely, this commandment that I am commanding you today is not too hard'), a text used by Paul in Romans 10. And the author's longing to 'speak face to face' (2 John 12; 3 John 14) might evoke the statement that God used to speak to Moses 'face to face'.

6

Conclusion

In our study of the later writings of the New Testament, we have seen numerous examples of what we might call traditional uses of Scripture, along with material that appears to be innovative. Thus certain texts, such as Genesis 15—22, Psalms 2, 110 and 118, and Isaiah 6—8 and 40—55 are used by various authors to support the death and resurrection of Christ and the resulting division between those who believe and those who do not. Other texts, such as Deuteronomy 18 and 32, Psalms 8 and 22, Proverbs 3 and Daniel 7 are present in specific strands of the tradition, such as Acts/Hebrews or Gospels/Revelation. Although it is difficult to decide whether Luke had sources for his early speeches or simply wrote what he thought was 'typical' of early preaching, it is likely that these were among the texts in use. Put another way, if Luke has simply put into the mouths of the apostles the texts that were being used in his day, then what texts did they use? Once it is granted that in seeking to proclaim the gospel in Jerusalem and the synagogues they would have almost certainly turned to the Scriptures, it would be difficult to argue that the texts they used were substantially different to the ones Luke has included.

I made a similar argument in *Jesus and Scripture*. Some scholars think that Jesus had no interest in Scripture and so all of the quotations attributed to him in the Gospels represent the teaching of the early Church.[1] However, this makes Jesus an anachronistic figure in the Jewish world. Once we grant that a Jewish teacher like Jesus is likely to have discussed and debated Scripture with his fellow Jews, then the question arises, which texts did he use if not the ones mentioned in the

145

Gospels? This is not to say that every text attributed to Jesus is necessarily genuine, since the New Testament authors were also capable of innovation and some of these texts might have been placed on his lips.[2] But there is no reason to dispute that the origin of the early Church's use of texts like Psalms 22, 110 and 118, and Isaiah 6 lie in Jesus' own use of them.

As well as following tradition, we have seen many examples of innovation. This takes several forms. The simplest is where the author draws on a traditional text but uses a different part of it. For example, Psalm 110.1 is quoted in the Gospels and Acts but only Hebrews takes up verse 4 ('You are a priest for ever according to the order of Melchizedek'). According to Matthew and Mark, Jesus' final words on the cross come from Psalm 22.1 ('My God, my God, why have you forsaken me?') but only Hebrews quotes from verse 22 ('I will tell of your name to my brothers and sisters; in the midst of the congregation I will praise you'). Similarly, Psalm 2.7 ('You are my son') is quoted in the Gospels, Acts and Hebrews but only Revelation draws on verse 9 ('You shall break them with a rod of iron') to describe the messianic victory. And Isaiah 40 is much quoted in the New Testament but only James and 1 Peter make use of verses 6–8 ('All people are grass'). It seems that specific quotations in the tradition led to the use of neighbouring texts.

Second, we see other texts in use that appear to have been suggested because they share either a common theme or specific wording. For example, the 'stone' text of Psalm 118.22 seems to have generated other 'stone' texts (Isa. 8.14, 28.16), while the 'subjection of enemies' theme in Psalm 110.1 has led to the 'subjection of creation' theme in Psalm 8.4–6 (Heb. 2.6–8; 1 Cor. 15.27). It was noted in *Jesus and Scripture* that the evidence that Jesus applied Isaiah 53 to himself is very slight. There are no quotations in Matthew and Mark and so the evidence turns on whether phrases like 'ransom for many' (Mark 10.45) and 'poured out for many' (Mark 14.24) are sufficient to evoke Isaiah 53.11–12. There is a short quotation in Luke 22.37 ('And he was counted among the lawless'), though this says nothing about a vicarious death on behalf of others. The two main passages in the New Testament where the text is quoted are Acts 8.32–33 and 1 Peter 2.22–25, both written some 30 to 50 years after Jesus' death. Thus a plausible scenario is that Jesus identified with various suffering figures (rejected stone, smitten shepherd, forsaken David) but once Jesus' death came to be understood as a sacrifice, attention was directed to Isaiah 53. This has not greatly influenced Matthew and Mark but Luke has the Ethiopian eunuch explicitly reading from this text and Jesus quoting the part about dying among criminals. Alternatively, it could be that the phrases in Mark are allusions to Isaiah 53 and this led to the developments that we now find in Luke–Acts and 1 Peter.[3]

Other connections depend on particular Greek words, such as God resting (*katepausen*) in Genesis 2.2 and the 'rest' (*katapausis*) promised in Psalm 95.11. This seems odd to us since the texts come from quite different contexts but it was a regular practice in Jewish interpretation (known by the Hebrew phrase, *gezerah shewa*). The assumption was that every word of Scripture was inspired by God and so must have an important meaning or function; it was the task of the exegete to discover it. The use of Psalm 16 as a proof-text for the resurrection is an interesting case in point: did it originate with Jesus or was it discovered later by Luke? There is good evidence that Jesus made reference to Psalm 110.1 (Mark 10.36; 14.62) and this explains Peter's use of it in his Pentecost speech. But there is no evidence that Jesus ever referred to Psalm 16 and its only occurrence in the New Testament is in the speeches of Peter and Paul. There are three main possibilities: (1) It was part of what Jesus communicated to the disciples after the resurrection; (2) It was an innovation of Peter and then used by Paul in his Antioch speech but not in any of his letters or elsewhere in the New Testament; (3) It was an innovation of Luke and placed on the lips of Peter and Paul. Most scholars favour the third as the first is a matter of speculation and if the second is true, one might have expected Paul to use it in his chapter on the resurrection (1 Corinthians 15).

Third, we see authors drawing on extra-biblical traditions to supply what is missing in Old Testament stories. Thus the flood was caused by 'fallen angels' leaving their place in heaven to have sex with human women (Jude 6). They are currently being held in chains until the day of judgement (2 Pet. 2.4). In Revelation, the persecution of Christians is a result of Satan being cast out of heaven (Rev. 12.7–17). Jude knows the story of Michael disputing with the devil over the body of Moses (Jude 9) and 2 Peter knows the proverb that the 'sow is washed only to wallow in the mud' (2 Pet. 2.22). For the author of Hebrews, the law was a *shadow* of the good things to come and not the true form of these realities (Heb. 10.1). The important point in all of this is that the Scriptures did not exist in a vacuum. They were part of a living tradition where text and interpretation were transmitted together. That is why the extremely useful *Commentary on the New Testament Use of the Old Testament* investigates each passage under the headings: (A) New Testament context; (B) Old Testament context; (C) Jewish background; (D) textual background; (E) author's use of the text; (F) theological use of the text. To echo the words of John Donne, no text is an island.

As for textual background, it is clear that Acts, 1 Peter and Hebrews take their quotations from Greek texts. They are generally fairly close to the major manuscripts that have come down to us, although there are differences and occasionally the interpretation depends on it (e.g. Edom/Adam in Acts 15.16–17). These might be explained by the author's lapse of memory, the use of a variant text or a deliberate alteration. The discovery of the Dead Sea Scrolls has made the second quite likely but there are cases where deliberate change is the best explanation. With Jude, 2 Peter and Revelation, it is much more difficult to say what type of text was being used because their method is mainly to allude to texts rather than quote them. There are some texts in Revelation, particularly from Ezekiel, which seem to depend on a Hebrew text, but other allusions show knowledge of the Greek.[4] Given the visionary nature of the book, this is not really surprising.

In conclusion, what we see in the later writings of the New Testament is both tradition and innovation. Some texts turn up again and again while others occur only in the one document. It could be likened to a musician who has first to learn the basic scales but then has the freedom to improvise. Although it is something of a generalization, the use of Scripture in Acts, James and 1 Peter is probably more tradition than innovation, while in Hebrews and Revelation it is more innovation than tradition. In Jude and 2 Peter, it is almost all innovation and represents a distinctive stream of thought in the New Testament. Some would like to see in the New Testament a model for how Scripture should be interpreted today. Our study has shown that such a model would have to embrace both tradition and innovation, and – for some at least – that is why it continues to be a fascinating area of study.

Appendix

Index of quotations in the later writings of the New Testament (UBS)

Acts		13.22a	Ps. 89.20
1.20a	Ps. 69.25	13.22b	1 Sam. 13.14
1.20b	Ps. 109.8	13.33	Ps. 2.7
2.17–21	Joel 2.28–32	13.34	Isa. 55.3
2.25–28	Ps. 16.8–11	13.35	Ps. 16.10
2.30	Ps. 132.11	13.41	Hab. 1.5
2.31	Ps. 16.10	13.47	Isa. 49.6
2.34–35	Ps. 110.1	15.16–17	Amos 9.11–12
3.13	Exod. 3.6, 15	23.5	Exod. 22.28
3.22	Deut. 18.15–16	28.26–27	Isa. 6.9–10
3.23a	Deut. 18.19		
3.23b	Lev. 23.29	**Hebrews**	
3.25	Gen. 22.18; 26.4	1.5a	Ps. 2.7
4.11	Ps. 118.22	1.5b	2 Sam. 7.14
4.25–26	Ps. 2.1–2	1.6	Deut. 32.43
7.3	Gen. 12.1	1.7	Ps. 104.4
7.5	Gen. 17.8; 48.4	1.8–9	Ps. 45.6–7
7.6–7	Gen. 15.13–14	1.10–12	Ps. 102.25–27
7.7	Exod. 3.12	1.13	Ps. 110.1
7.18	Exod. 1.8	2.6–8	Ps. 8.4–6
7.27–28	Exod. 2.14	2.12	Ps. 22.22
7.30	Exod. 3.2	2.13a	Isa. 8.17
7.32	Exod. 3.6	2.13b	Isa. 8.18
7.33	Exod. 3.5	3.7–11	Ps. 95.7–11
7.34	Exod. 3.7, 8, 10	3.15	Ps. 95.7–8
7.35	Exod. 2.14	4.3, 5	Ps. 95.11
7.37	Deut. 18.15	4.4	Gen. 2.2
7.40	Exod. 32.1, 23	4.7	Ps. 95.7–8
7.42–43	Amos 5.25–27	5.5	Ps. 2.7
7.49–50	Isa. 66.1–2	5.6	Ps. 110.4
8.32–33	Isa. 53.7–8	6.13–14	Gen. 22.16–17

Notes

Introduction

1 Steve Moyise, *Paul and Scripture* (London: SPCK/Grand Rapids, MI: Baker Academic, 2010); *Jesus and Scripture* (London: SPCK, 2010; Grand Rapids, MI: Baker Academic, 2011).

2 J. B. Green, S. McKnight and I. H. Marshall (eds), *Dictionary of Jesus and the Gospels* (Downers Grove, IL; InterVarsity Press, 1992); G. F. Hawthorne, R. P. Martin and D. G. Reid (eds), *Dictionary of Paul and his Letters* (Downers Grove, IL; InterVarsity Press, 1993); R. P. Martin and P. Davids (eds), *Dictionary of the Later New Testament and its Developments* (Downers Grove, IL; InterVarsity Press, 1997). In terms of quantity, the Gospels occupy 47 per cent of the New Testament and the Pauline corpus 22 per cent, leaving around 31 per cent for the remaining authors.

3 S. Moyise, *The Old Testament in the New: An Introduction* (London: T. & T. Clark, 2001).

1 Acts and Scripture

1 Early tradition associates the authorship of the third Gospel and Acts with the Luke mentioned in Colossians 4.14, 2 Timothy 4.11 and Philemon 24. From this distance, we cannot tell if they had any evidence for this or were making an educated guess based on passages like Acts 16.11, where the narrative changes to 'We set sail'. There is an even greater difficulty with identifying Theophilus, since the name means 'lover of God' and could be intended as symbolic. The majority of scholars think that a particular individual is in mind, though it is likely that Luke also has a wider readership in view. Although certainty is impossible, most scholars think that Theophilus was a Gentile.

2 Though the phrase 'last days' has been inserted into the Joel quotation, which simply says 'Then afterward'.

3 Not all agree that the fate of the Gentiles in Joel 3 is decisive for the meaning of 'all flesh' and 'everyone who calls' in Joel 2. James

A. Meek, in *The Gentile Mission in Old Testament Citations in Acts* (LNTS, 385; London and New York: T. & T. Clark, 2008), says: 'While the focus is on Judah, the promises must include faithful Jews in the Diaspora (on the one hand) and Gentile slaves and sojourners in Judah (on the other)... Gifts of the Spirit and deliverance will be shared by Gentiles who, in the future as in Israel's past, call on the name of Yahweh because they have been called by him' (p. 104).

4 The Hebrew verb can be taken as passive 'be blessed' or reflexive 'bless oneself' but the LXX is definitely passive ('be blessed') and this is what we find in Acts.

5 Meek, *The Gentile Mission*, p. 53.

6 I quote from the RSV here because the inclusive language of the NRSV renders the phrase 'all other peoples', which obscures the connection between *edom* ('Edom') and *adam* ('men/humanity'). The words for 'possess' and 'seek' in Hebrew are *yarash* and *darash*.

7 Meek (*The Gentile Mission*, pp. 56–94) argues that the phrase that supports James's point is 'all the Gentiles who are called by my name', which is present in both the Greek and the Hebrew. This points to the full inclusion of the Gentiles and it may be that the LXX changed the earlier part of the verse in order to make this more explicit.

8 Charles Kingsley Barrett, *A Critical and Exegetical Commentary on the Acts of the Apostles Vol 1* (ICC; Edinburgh: T. & T. Clark, 1994), pp. 229–30.

9 The Hebrew uses the word *nephesh* to refer to a person (Gen. 2.7), which the LXX frequently renders *psychē*. However, in Greek philosophy, *psychē* can refer to that which is immortal, hence the English translation 'soul'. *Hades* is the usual translation of *sheol* but perhaps adds a note of punishment. *Hasid* means 'pious, faithful, devout', but 'holy' is an acceptable rendering. The most difficult to explain is rendering *shahat* ('pit') with *diaphthora* ('corruption'), though there is a very similar Hebrew word meaning 'destruction', which might have prompted the rendering.

10 The standard work is Leonard Goppelt, *Typos: The Typological Interpretation of the Old Testament in the New* (Grand Rapids, MI: Eerdmans, 1982). See also Jon Whitman, *Interpretation and Allegory:*

Antiquity to the Modern Period (Leiden: Brill, 2000) and Frances W. Young, *Biblical Exegesis and the Formation of Christian Culture* (Cambridge: Cambridge University Press, 1997).

11 For a discussion of which quotations can be said to go back to Jesus, see the companion volume, Steve Moyise, *Jesus and Scripture* (London: SPCK, 2010; Grand Rapids, MI: Baker Academic, 2011).

12 Barrett, *Acts*, pp. 151–2. The opposite view is expressed by I. Howard Marshall in *The Acts of the Apostles: An Introduction and Commentary* (Leicester: Inter-Varsity Press, 1980), p. 77: 'Peter's argument obviously does not mean that Jesus *became* Messiah by being raised from the dead, but rather that since the Messiah must rise from the dead, and since Jesus rose from the dead, it follows that Jesus was already the Messiah during his earthly life.'

13 This is part of the Prayer of Azariah, included in the Catholic edition of the NRSV between Daniel 3.23 and 24. It represents an expansion of the Hebrew Daniel and is present in the LXX.

14 The Hebrew as represented by the NRSV says: 'See, my servant shall prosper; he shall be exalted and lifted up, and shall be very high.'

15 Peter Mallen, *The Reading and Transformation of Isaiah in Luke–Acts* (LNTS, 367; London and New York: T. & T. Clark, 2008), p. 126.

16 Peter Doble, 'The Psalms in Luke–Acts' in Steve Moyise and Maarten J. J. Menken (eds), *The Psalms in the New Testament* (London and New York: T. & T. Clark, 2004), pp. 83–117, at p. 104.

17 Barrett, *Acts*, p. 645. The Masoretic Text understands the Hebrew consonants *nwr'* to derive from *yr'* ('fear'), whereas the LXX appears to have derived them from *r'h* ('see'), and hence 'manifest'.

18 A different type of change is found in Matthew 2.6, where Micah 5.2 is quoted to show that Bethlehem is 'by no means least among the rulers of Judah'. Readers who look up the verse will be surprised to find that Matthew has inserted the phrase 'by no means' (one word in Greek) into the quotation. Micah asserts that Bethlehem is the least.

19 If 'traitors' was original, the LXX's 'scoffers' is weaker but understandable and the Masoretic Text can be explained as a misreading

of the consonants for 'traitors' (*bwgdym*) for the phrase 'at the nations' (*bgwym*). It is harder to explain the LXX's 'perish'. The Hebrew uses an idiom where the verb is repeated (lit. 'be amazed, be amazed') which is a way of intensifying the action. The NRSV uses two different words ('Be astonished! Be astounded!') to express this whereas the NIV goes for intensification: 'be utterly amazed'. The LXX reproduces the idiom (*'thaumasate thaumasia'*) but adds another word (*aphanisthēte*), which means 'disappear' or 'perish'. Texts from the Dead Sea Scrolls are taken from Geza Vermes, *The Complete Dead Sea Scrolls in English* (London: Penguin, 1997).

20 In Chris Stanley's work on Paul, he challenges those who assume that the churches would have easy access to LXX scrolls or that many would have been able to read them anyway. Similarly, while Luke could probably assume that Theophilus was acquainted with those passages frequently quoted by Christians (Genesis 15; Exodus 20; Deuteronomy 32; Isaiah 40—55; Pss. 2, 69, 110, 118), it is doubtful he would know Habakkuk 1.5, which is not otherwise quoted in the New Testament, or would have easy access to it. See Christopher D. Stanley, *Arguing with Scripture: The Rhetoric of Quotations in the Letters of Paul* (New York and London: T. & T. Clark, 2004).

21 Barrett, *Acts*, p. 138.

22 Barrett, *Acts*, p. 374.

23 F. F. Bruce, *Commentary on the Book of the Acts: The English Text with Introduction, Exposition and Notes* (London: Marshall, Morgan and Scott, 1965), p. 159.

24 Barrett, *Acts*, p. 373.

25 Mallen, *Isaiah in Luke–Acts*, p. 116.

26 Kenneth Litwak, *Echoes of Scripture in Luke–Acts: Telling the History of God's People Intertextually* (JSNTSup, 282; London and New York: T. & T. Clark, 2005).

27 Some manuscripts (D it) say that it is written in the first psalm and suggest that in some versions of the Psalter, the first two psalms were taken as a single psalm.

28 Peter Doble, 'Luke 24.26, 44 – Songs of God's Servant: David and his Psalms in Luke–Acts', *JSNT* 28 (2006), pp. 267–83.

29 Doble, 'Songs of God's Servant', p. 275.
30 David W. Pao, *Acts and the Isaianic New Exodus* (WUNT, 2.130; Tübingen: Mohr Siebeck, 2000).
31 Mallen, *Isaiah in Luke–Acts*, p. 189.
32 Mallen, *Isaiah in Luke–Acts*, p. 207.
33 Mallen is drawing on my chapter 'Intertextuality and the Study of the Old Testament in the New' in Steve Moyise (ed.), *The Old Testament in the New Testament* (JSNTSup, 189; Sheffield: Sheffield Academic Press, 2000), pp. 14–41.
34 Mallen, *Isaiah in Luke–Acts*, p. 205.
35 Mark has Jesus ending his life with words from Psalm 22.1 ('My God, my God, why have you forsaken me?') but Luke uses a different psalm ('Father, into your hands I commend my spirit' – Ps. 31.5).

2 1 Peter and Scripture

1 It is clear that the letter purports to come from the apostle, both from the introduction in 2 Peter 1.1 ('Simeon Peter, a servant and apostle of Jesus Christ') and the claim to be an eyewitness in 1.16–18.
2 The following chapter draws on Steve Moyise, *Evoking Scripture: Seeing the Old Testament in the New* (London and New York: Continuum, 2008), pp. 78–95.
3 M. Eugene Boring, *1 Peter* (Nashville: Abingdon Press, 1999), p. 94.
4 Karen H. Jobes, *1 Peter* (BECNT; Grand Rapids, MI: Baker Academic, 2005), p. 223. She also notes that the LXX translation of verse 4 of the psalm 'and from all my sojournings he delivered me' would have appealed to the author and offers a parallel to 1 Peter 1.17 (lit. 'in fear live out your time of sojourning').
5 Jobes, *1 Peter*, p. 126.
6 John H. Elliott, *1 Peter* (AB, 38B; New York: Doubleday, 2000), p. 391.
7 J. Ramsey Michaels, *1 Peter* (WBC, 49; Dallas, TX: Word Books, 1988), p. 79.
8 The presence of 'and if anyone trusts in him' in the LXX of Isaiah 8.14, without a basis in the Hebrew text, already suggests a link with Isaiah 28.16 in the eyes of the LXX translators. Indeed, it is

possible that the Qumran document 1QS 8.4ff. offers evidence for a link between the Hebrew texts.

9 W. L. Schutter, *Hermeneutics and Composition in 1 Peter* (WUNT, 2.30; Tübingen: Mohr Siebeck, 1989), p. 136.

10 The quotation follows the LXX where it is God's mighty acts (*aretas*) that are proclaimed, rather than his 'praises'.

11 So Leonard Goppelt, *A Commentary on 1 Peter* (trans. J. E. Alsup; Grand Rapids, MI: Eerdmans, 1993). In favour is the link between Isaiah 6.10 and 53.1 in John 12.38–40 and the fact that *epistrephō* does not occur in Isaiah 53 or again in 1 Peter. On the other hand, it is an extremely common word (*c.* 500 in LXX) and Ramsey Michaels (*1 Peter*, p. 150) thinks it is just as likely that it was suggested by the metaphor of sheep going astray.

12 So Elliott, *1 Peter*, p. 538. The metaphor of God's flock straying and returning might seem incongruous for a Gentile audience but it appears to apply to their previous alienation from God.

13 D. A. Carson, '1 Peter' in Greg K. Beale and Dan A. Carson (eds), *Commentary on the New Testament Use of the Old Testament* (Grand Rapids, MI: Baker Academic, 2007), p. 1038.

14 Most translations split 'Lord' and 'Christ' and render the phrase as either sanctify, reverence or set apart 'Christ as Lord'. However, as Carson notes ('1 Peter', p. 1038), the verb *hagiazō* is never used in the sense of 'revering X as Y' and so we really need to keep Lord and Christ together. The NJB does this though its rendering ('proclaim the Lord Christ holy in your hearts') is somewhat obscure. The scribal answer was to change 'Christ' to 'God' and hence the KJV reads: 'sanctify the Lord God in your hearts.'

15 Boring, *1 Peter*, p. 174.

16 Edward G. Selwyn, *The First Epistle of St. Peter* (London: Macmillan, 1947), p. 460.

17 Carson ('1 Peter', p. 1017) notes how the text was important to the Qumran community, using such terms as 'holy community' (1QSa 1.12–13), 'holy council' (1QS 2.25) and 'holy fellowship' (1QS 9.2).

18 Goppelt, *1 Peter*, pp. 255–63.

19 A good exposition of this view is Jobes, *1 Peter*, pp. 242–60.

20 The interpretation of 'sons of God' in Genesis 6.2 as angels is found in *1 Enoch* (6—19, 21, 86—88), *Jubilees* (4.15, 22; 5.1), *The Testaments of the Twelve Patriarchs* (*T. Reub.* 5.6–7; *T. Naph.* 3.5), *2 Baruch* (56.10–14) and the Dead Sea Scrolls (CD-A II, 17–19; 1QapGen II, 1). Later rabbinic tradition became unhappy with this interpretation and took 'sons of God' to mean 'men'.

21 For the texts, see James H. Charlesworth (ed.), *The Old Testament Pseudepigrapha Vol 1: Apocalyptic Literature and Testaments* (London: Darton, Longman and Todd, 1983).

22 Selwyn, *The First Epistle of St. Peter*, p. 136.

23 Another possibility is that the *eis christon* should be taken in a temporal sense, meaning 'sufferings until Christ'. A parallel would be Galatians 3.24, where the law is said to be 'our disciplinarian until Christ came (*eis christon*)'. The meaning in 1 Peter would then be the sum total of the sufferings of God's people, from the prophet's own time to the time of Christ. The difficulty of this is that it would seem to exclude or at least play down the actual sufferings of Christ ('until Christ').

24 Anthony T. Hanson, *The Living Utterances of God* (London: Darton, Longman and Todd, 1983), p. 141.

25 Jobes, *1 Peter*, p. 101.

26 Galatians: Genesis 12.3, 7; 15.6; 18.18; 21.10; Leviticus 18.5; 19.18; Deuteronomy 21.23; 27.26; Isaiah 54.1; Habakkuk 2.4.
   2 Corinthians: Exodus 16.18; Leviticus 26.12; Deuteronomy 19.15; 2 Samuel 7.8, 14; Psalms 112.9; 116.10; Isaiah 49.8; Ezekiel 20.34; 37.27; Jeremiah 9.24.

3 Jude, 2 Peter and James and Scripture

1 There is no doubt that 2 Peter claims to come from Peter, both from the opening verse, the claim in 2 Peter 1.16–18 that he was present at the transfiguration, and the reference in 2 Peter 3.1 that this is his second letter to them. For recent discussion of the evidence, see Gene L. Green, *Jude and 2 Peter* (BECNT; Grand Rapids, MI: Baker Academic, 2008) and Peter H. Davids, *The Letters of 2 Peter and Jude* (PNTC; Grand Rapids, MI: Eerdmans, 2006).

2 For a recent discussion of the evidence, see Scot McKnight, *The Letter of James* (NICNT; Grand Rapids, MI: Eerdmans, 2011);

Dan G. McCartney, *James* (BECNT; Grand Rapids, MI: Baker, 2009); Douglas J. Moo, *The Letter of James* (PNTC; Grand Rapids, MI: Eerdmans, 2000). Also valuable are Luke T. Johnson, *The Letter of James: A New Translation with Introduction and Commentary* (AB, 37A; New York: Doubleday, 1995) and Richard J. Bauckham, *James: Wisdom of James, Disciple of Jesus the Sage* (New York: Routledge, 1999).

3 For Dan Carson, the point is that 'just because people belong to the right community does not mean that they can escape the judgment of God'; see 'Jude' in Greg K. Beale and Dan A. Carson (eds), *Commentary on the New Testament Use of the Old Testament* (Grand Rapids, MI: Baker Academic, 2007), p. 1070.

4 Richard J. Bauckham, *Jude, 2 Peter* (WBC, 50; Waco, TX: Word, 1983), p. 54. In the Old Testament, the sin of Sodom is said to be injustice (Isa. 1.10; 3.9), pride (Ezek. 16.48–50) or apostasy (Jer. 23.14). In later Jewish tradition, it was generally thought to be a violation of hospitality (Wisd. 19.14–15; Josephus, *Jewish Antiquities*, 1.194). It is Philo (*On the Life of Abraham*, 135–36) who understands it as homosexuality.

5 See the lengthy excursus in Bauckham, *Jude, 2 Peter*, pp. 65–76, where the text of the Slavonic *Life of Moses* is quoted: 'For the devil contended with the angel, and would not permit his body to be buried, saying, "Moses is a murderer. He slew a man in Egypt and hid him in the sand." Then Michael prayed to God and there was thunder and lightning and suddenly the devil disappeared; but Michael buried him with his (own) hands' (p. 69). Bauckham believes that Jude used a version of the *Testament of Moses* that was later revised and known as the *Assumption of Moses*.

6 'I overthrew some of you, as when God overthrew Sodom and Gomorrah, and you were like a brand snatched from the fire; yet you did not return to me, says the Lord' (Amos 4.11).

7 The verb used here is *tartaroun*, which literally means, 'to throw into Tartarus', the place where the Cyclopes and Titans were imprisoned in Greek mythology. This does not in itself mean that the author is aware of Hesiod's *Theogony*, for the noun *tartaros* has also found its way into the LXX of Job 40.20, 41.24 and Proverbs 30.16.

8 The connection here is not in fact the English word 'blemishes' but the word translated 'spots'. Jude used the obscure word *spilades*, which literally means 'dangerous reef' (NJB: 'They are a dangerous hazard at your community meals'). It seems that 2 Peter was puzzled by this and used *spiloi* ('spots') instead, probably because the goal of the Christian life, according to 2 Peter 3.14, is to be *aspiloi* ('without spot').

9 Bauckham, *Jude, 2 Peter*, p. 279.

10 It uses a different word from the LXX for 'return', 'its own' and 'vomit' and differs from both Greek and Hebrew in omitting the initial comparison 'like a dog'.

11 So Peter Enns, *Inspiration and Incarnation: Evangelicals and the Problem of the Old Testament* (Grand Rapids, MI: Baker Academic, 2005).

12 This is particularly so with a book like *1 Enoch*, which clearly combines a variety of sources. As Carson puts it, 'if Jude overlaps in content with one element found in, say *1 Enoch*, it does not necessarily follow that Jude buys into all that *1 Enoch* says on the subject'; see Carson, 'Jude' in Beale and Carson (eds), *New Testament Use of the Old Testament*, p. 1069.

13 McKnight, *James*, p. 218.

14 There is a possible criticism of the law in James 5.12: 'Above all, my beloved, do not swear, either by heaven or by earth or by any other oath, but let your "Yes" be yes and your "No" be no, so that you may not fall under condemnation.' But this corresponds to Jesus' teaching in Matthew 5.34 and may indeed be a more primitive form of the tradition.

15 See Scott H. Hendrix, *Martin Luther: A Very Short Introduction* (Oxford: Oxford University Press, 2010).

16 Patrick J. Hartin, *A Spirituality of Perfection: Faith in Action in the Letter of James* (Collegeville, MN: Liturgical Press, 1999), p. 89.

17 Robert W. Wall, *Community of the Wise: The Letter of James* (Valley Forge, PA: Trinity Press International, 1997). See also Bauckham, *James*.

18 Other possible allusions are the early and late rains in James 5.7 (Jer. 5.24; Joel 2.23) and oppressing the hired workers, orphans and widows in James 5.4 (Mal. 3.5).

4 Hebrews and Scripture

1 Simon Kistemaker, *The Psalm Citations in the Epistle to the Hebrews* (Amsterdam: van Soest, 1961); Dirk J. Human and Gert J. Steyn (eds), *Psalms and Hebrews: Studies in Reception* (LHB, 527; New York and London: T. & T. Clark, 2010).

2 There are no early references to the authorship of the book. Clement of Alexandria suggested that Paul wrote it in Hebrew and Luke translated it, but there is little to commend this. Tertullian suggested Barnabas, perhaps because of its priestly interests. Eventually, it came to be thought of as the work of Paul, but few modern scholars support this. Not only does it lack many of Paul's key themes (indwelling of the Spirit, being 'in Christ', justification), its central idea of Christ as High Priest does not figure in Paul's writings.

3 Graham R. Hughes, *Hebrews and Hermeneutics* (Cambridge: Cambridge University Press, 1979), p. 12.

4 Psalm 2.7 (Acts 13.33 + Jesus' baptism); 2 Samuel 7.14 (2 Cor. 6.18; Rev. 21.7); Deuteronomy 32.43 (Rom. 15.10, though a different part of the verse); Psalm 110.1 (Matt. 22.44; 26.64 and parallels; Acts 2.34; 1 Cor. 15.25).

5 Herbert W. Bateman, *Early Jewish Hermeneutics and Hebrews 1.5–13* (New York: Peter Lang, 1979), p. 241.

6 The words are in fact printed in the NRSV with the footnote: 'Q Ms Gk: MT lacks this line.' What this means is that the reading is not only present in the LXX (=Gk) but also in a Hebrew manuscript discovered at Qumran (4QDeut^q). The NRSV has decided that this is sufficient evidence to conclude that it originally belonged to the Hebrew text even though it is missing from the Masoretic Text. An exact parallel is found in a work known as *Odes* (2.43), a collection of hymns attached to the Psalter in the fifth-century Codex Alexandrinus. Some scholars think this evidence is too late to be a serious contender but Gert Steyn supports it.

7 Hugh W. Montefiore, *The Epistle to the Hebrews* (London: A. & C. Black, 1964), pp. 42–50.

8 Harold W. Attridge, *The Epistle to the Hebrews* (Hermeneia Commentaries; Philadelphia: Fortress Press, 1989), pp. 50–1. He thinks the author probably added the quotations from Psalms 45, 102

and 104 because they 'do not appear elsewhere in any messianic
or exaltation context and give expression to important themes of
Hebrews and its christology' (p. 50).

9 Susan E. Docherty, *The Use of the Old Testament in Hebrews*
(WUNT, 2.260; Tübingen: Mohr Siebeck, 2009), p. 181.

10 There is debate as to whether the Hebrew *elohim* is a reference to
God or the plural form is being used to refer to 'gods' (Ps. 82.1, 6),
or specifically angels (Ps. 97.7). It is noteworthy that the Aramaic
Targum takes it to mean 'angels' and so the LXX may be correct.

11 George H. Guthrie, 'Hebrews' in G. K. Beale and D. A. Carson (eds),
Commentary on the New Testament Use of the Old Testament (Grand
Rapids, MI: Baker Academic, 2007), pp. 919–95 at p. 946.

12 Most translations assume that Hebrews is exploiting this ambiguity and render the phrase 'a little while'. However, the NIV follows
the KJV and simply renders 'a little lower'.

13 The title of Psalm 92 is 'A Song for the Sabbath Day' and in the
psalms that follow, there is a particular emphasis on creation.
In later Jewish tradition, Psalm 95 was one of the psalms read
on the eve of the Sabbath. See Christian Frevel, '*Semeron* –
Understanding Psalm 95 Within, and Without, Hebrews' in
Human and Steyn (eds), *Psalms and Hebrews*, pp. 165–93 at
pp. 188–9.

14 Attridge, *Hebrews*, p. 123. It used to be thought that the author
made up the word *sabbatismos* since this is its first occurrence in
all Greek literature. However, Attridge (p. 131) notes that it occurs
in Plutarch, who was hardly dependent on Hebrews.

15 Paul Ellingworth, *The Epistle to the Hebrews: A Commentary on
the Greek Text* (Grand Rapids, MI: Eerdmans/Carlisle: Paternoster
Press, 1993), p. 49.

16 George W. Buchanan, *To the Hebrews: Translation, Comments and
Conclusions* (AB, 36; New York: Doubleday, 1972).

17 Gert J. C. Jordaan and Pieter Nel, 'From Priest-King to King-Priest:
Psalm 110 and the Basic Structure of Hebrews' in Human and
Steyn (eds), *Psalms and Hebrews*, pp. 229–40.

18 In addition, the quotation in Hebrews 10.16–18 uses a pronoun
('them') for 'the house of Israel' and reduces the two clauses in 'For
I will be merciful towards their iniquities, and I will remember

their sins no more' to 'I will remember their sins and their lawless deeds no more'.

19 See Femi Adeyemi, *The New Covenant Torah in Jeremiah and the Law of Christ in Paul* (New York: Peter Lang, 2006).

20 Ellingworth, *Hebrews*, p. 413.

21 The parallels have led some scholars to suggest that the author of Hebrews is specifically drawing on Philo but others have pointed out that the differences far outweigh the similarities. For a brief survey, see the excursus on 'The Heavenly Temple and its Significance' in Attridge, *Hebrews*, pp. 222–4.

22 Martin Karrer, 'LXX Psalm 39:7–10 in Hebrews 10:5–7' in Steyn and Human (eds), *Psalms and Hebrews*, pp. 126–46, at p. 130.

23 It has frequently been argued that the word 'body' is so crucial to the argument of Hebrews that it is more likely that it has influenced the extant LXX manuscripts (which all post-date Hebrews) than the other way around. Indeed, in the version of the LXX edited by Rahlfs, the word 'ears' is printed, despite the fact that 'body' is found in every Greek manuscript ('ears' is found in some Latin manuscripts). Karrer is one scholar who regards this as mistaken, noting that Papyrus Bodmer 24 (our earliest witness to the LXX text of the psalm and unknown to Rahlfs) also reads 'body' ('LXX Psalm 39:7–10', pp. 140–5).

24 'Let them see your zeal for your people, and be ashamed. Let the fire for your adversaries consume them' (Isa. 26.11). As well as the common words 'fire' and 'consume', Hebrews 10.27 also uses *zēlos* ('zeal') for God's fury and the adjective *hupenantios* ('opposed') for 'adversaries' (the only such usage in the New Testament).

25 The Hebrew uses two nouns ('vengeance is mine and recompense') while the LXX has 'in a day of vengeance, I will repay'. Paul uses the text to warn Christians from taking vengeance since that is the prerogative of God.

26 Attridge, *Hebrews*, p. 296. For the importance of the Song of Moses in Hebrews, see David M. Allen, *Deuteronomy and Exhortation in Hebrews* (Tübingen: Mohr Siebeck, 2007).

27 Richard B. Hays, *Echoes of Scripture in the Letters of Paul* (New Haven, CT: Yale University Press, 1989), pp. 33–44.

28 Although such changes sound gratuitous, it is likely that later copyists simply assumed that an earlier copyist had introduced an error and they were correcting it – in this case, back to the LXX. If this is correct, then the LXX reading found in the fifth-century Codex Alexandrinus ('my righteous') has been influenced by Hebrews. On the other hand, the great majority of Byzantine manuscripts of Hebrews omit the pronoun altogether and this was followed by the KJV ('the just shall live by faith'). This is almost certainly a case of conforming the reading to Romans 1.17 and Galatians 3.11.

29 Radu Gheorghita, *The Role of the Septuagint in Hebrews: An Investigation of its Influence with Special Consideration to the Use of Hab 2:3–4 in Heb 10:37–38* (Tübingen: Mohr Siebeck, 2003), p. 221.

30 Gheorghita, *The Role of the Septuagint in Hebrews*, p. 224.

31 The Greek verb is *elengchō*, which is used of John the Baptist 'reproving' Herod (Luke 3.19), the Holy Spirit 'convicting' the world of sin (John 16.8), evil deeds being 'exposed' (Eph. 5.11) and sinners 'rebuked' by their overseer (1 Tim. 5.20). In a number of these examples, the *result* of the rebuking/convicting/reproving might well be a 'punishment' but that does not seem to be the word's primary meaning. The NIV follows the KJV in rendering Hebrews 12.5 with 'rebuke'.

32 Philo, *On the Virtues*, 208, quoted in Attridge, *Hebrews*, p. 369.

33 Attridge (*Hebrews*, p. 370) says: 'As is frequently the case in Hebrews's handling of biblical stories, the paraenetic point, not the original plot, is determinative. A second repentance is simply not an object-ive possibility.'

34 NIV follows later manuscripts and adds 'mountain'.

35 Quoted in Hays, *Echoes of Scripture*, p. 142.

36 Attridge, *Hebrews*, p. 381.

5 Revelation and Scripture

1 Some scholars think that 1 Thessalonians represents the convic-tion of the early Church that Jesus would return soon (see 1 Cor. 7.25–31) but 2 Thessalonians comes from a much later period when this had not happened and requires some explanation. Those

who hold this view think that 2 Thessalonians was not written directly by Paul but written in his name by a later disciple.

2 There is a further option which takes the verb 'to see' in a metaphorical sense. John may have 'seen' things in Scripture and combined them with what he 'saw' in a vision. This is suggested by the fact that some of his visions are impossible to visualize, such as the dragon sweeping one third of the stars onto the earth (Rev. 12.4).

3 There is an oddity in the Greek grammar of Revelation 1.4 since the preposition *apo* ('from') should be followed by a genitive but the titles are all in the nominative. Some think this is for honorific reasons, the threefold title not subject to change like 'ordinary' nouns but Greg Beale thinks it is a deliberate pointer to the LXX of Exodus 3.14; see *The Book of Revelation* (NIGTC; Grand Rapids, MI: Eerdmans/Carlisle: Paternoster Press, 1999), p. 188.

4 Another important text is the LXX of Isaiah 11.2–3, where the Spirit of God is described by seven characteristics (the Hebrew only has six) and is cited by Justin and Irenaeus. The view that the seven spirits are the seven principal angels is held by David E. Aune, *Revelation 1—5* (WBC, 52A; Dallas, TX: Word Books, 1997), pp. 33–6.

5 George B. Caird, *The Revelation of St. John the Divine* (2nd edn; London: A. & C. Black, 1984), p. 75.

6 John 7.42 (Ps. 89.3–4); John 12.34 (Ps. 89.4, 36); Luke 1.51 (Ps. 89.10); 1 Cor. 10.26 (Ps. 89.11); 1 Pet. 1.17 (Ps. 89.26); 1 Pet. 4.14 (Ps. 89.50).

7 Grant R. Osborne, *Revelation* (BECNT; Grand Rapids, MI: Baker Academic, 2002), p. 69.

8 Caird, *Revelation of St. John*, p. 25. However, he does think the detail of Christ's appearance among the seven lampstands has specific theological meaning: 'He is no absentee, who has withdrawn from earth at his Ascension, to return only at his Parousia . . . The first characteristic of Christ revealed to John in his vision is that he is present among the earthly congregations of his people' (p. 25).

9 It is interesting that while most Greek manuscripts of Daniel 7.13 say that the one like a son of man comes 'unto' the Ancient of Days, there are a few that say he comes 'as' the Ancient of

Days. If John knew of such a tradition, it could explain how John merges the two figures in the inaugural vision but keeps them separate in Revelation 5. See Christopher C. Rowland, 'The Vision of the Risen Christ in Rev. 1.13ff.: The Debt of an Early Christology to an Aspect of Jewish Angelology', *JTS* (1980), pp. 1–11.

10 Peter R. Carrell, *Jesus and the Angels: Angelology and the Christology of the Apocalypse of John* (SNTSM, 95; Cambridge: Cambridge University Press, 1997), pp. 53–61. Thus in *1 Enoch* 14.20, God's raiment was 'brighter than the sun, and whiter than any snow', while in *1 Enoch* 71.1–2 the 'sons of the holy angels' have pure white garments and faces like snow (though these two passages probably come from different authors).

11 The 'son of man' expression and mention of a cloud link the figure with Daniel 7.13 and the inaugural vision and are favoured by Osborne and Beale. On the other hand, the next verse begins, 'Another angel came out of the temple' (14.15) and gives the one sitting on the cloud a command, suggesting that the figure is an angel (so David E. Aune, *Revelation 6—16* (WBC, 52B; Nashville, TN: Thomas Nelson, 1998)).

12 Robert L. Thomas, *Revelation 1—7: An Exegetical Commentary* (Chicago: Moody Press, 1992), pp. 341–4.

13 Osborne, *Revelation*, p. 227.

14 Josephine Massyngberde Ford, *Revelation: Introduction, Translation, and Commentary* (AB, 38; Garden City, NY: Doubleday, 1975), p. 31.

15 Richard Bauckham, in *The Climax of Prophecy: Studies on the Book of Revelation* (Edinburgh: T. & T. Clark, 1993), pp. 183–4, says that this verse has so obviously been rewritten if not entirely composed by a Christian editor that it cannot be used as evidence for a 'conquering lamb' tradition.

16 John L. Resseguie, *Revelation Unsealed: A Narrative Critical Approach to John's Apocalypse* (Leiden: Brill, 1998), p. 134.

17 Mark Bredin, *Jesus, Revolutionary of Peace: A Nonviolent Christology in the Book of Revelation* (Carlisle: Paternoster Press, 2003), p. 195.

18 Caird, *Revelation of St. John*, pp. 243–4.

19 Bauckham, *Climax of Prophecy*, p. 233.

20 In favour of the 'messianic community' interpretation are the following: (1) the woman is introduced as holding 12 stars, probably

an allusion to Jacob's dream in Genesis 37, which concerns the destiny of a people; (2) texts like Numbers 2.4, 9.14; Isaiah 60.19–20 apply this imagery to the faithful; (3) the unusual wording of 'she gave birth to a son, a male child' in 12.5 points to Isaiah 66.7 and the following verse suggests this is corporate; (4) the word used for her agony is *basanizō*, which is frequently used for the persecution of the faithful (over 60 times in 4 Maccabees) but never of literal birth pains; and (5) her protection in the wilderness evokes the wilderness wandering of Israel.

21 If it does refer to a particular individual, then 'Nero Caesar' is the most likely. If written in Hebrew letters, the total is 666 (or can be) and it might also explain why a few manuscripts have 616, which would be the total in Latin letters. However, it is unclear why John would adopt Hebrew letters and may be a later rationalization since Nero was known to persecute the Church.

22 Four verses in Proverbs (3.18; 11.30; 13.12; 15.4) compare some aspect of the wise or righteous to *a* tree of life but the meaning is generic. The same is true of Isaiah 65.22, though the LXX has made the reference definite ('according to the days of *the* tree of life shall the days of my people be'). The only other reference is Ezekiel 47.12, which is discussed on pages 137–9.

23 The mention of Gog and Magog in Revelation 20.8 could suggest that Ezekiel 37 was the catalyst, for it pictures a 'united kingdom' under a new David *prior* to the battle and defeat of Gog of the land of Magog. Daniel may also have contributed with his division of the time between the decree that the Jews could return to Jerusalem and the anointed one as seven weeks (of years), followed by 62 weeks and a final week (Dan. 10.24–27). *1 Enoch* 91—103 divides history into 10 weeks, the messianic kingdom being established on the eighth. Probably the first text to specifically cite the length of the reign is *4 Ezra* 7.26–30, where it is 400 years. Rabbi Eliezer ben Hyrcanus (*c.* 90 CE) appears to be the earliest text that gives 1000 years.

24 Austin Farrer, *The Revelation of St. John the Divine* (Oxford: Clarendon, 1964), p. 222.

25 The NRSV has a footnote that 'other ancient authorities read *people*'. It is a difficult textual decision since both readings have

good support and reasons can be offered for why a scribe might have changed the singular to the plural (to agree with the plural 'and they shall be') or the plural to the singular (to agree with the Old Testament). Whatever the original was, it is clear from Revelation 21.24 ('The nations will walk by its light, and the kings of the earth will bring their glory into it') that its meaning is inclusive.

26 Most of the early canon lists or manuscripts either omit the book altogether (Marcion, Cyril, Synod of Laodicea, *Apostolic Constitutions*, Gregory of Nazianzus, Peshitta [Syriac translation]) or end with something else (*Revelation to Peter* in the Muratorian Canon and Codex Claromontanus and Sirach in Epiphanius). In the Eastern Church, it was not until the eleventh century that it was established as the final book of the canon and it is still not recognized in the lectionary. For the Western Church, it was the festal letter of Athanasius in 367 CE and later endorsed by Augustine that established Revelation as the final book of the canon.

27 According to the list of quotations and allusions in UBS (pp. 879–911), the ratios of Pentateuch to Isaiah and Ezekiel are as follows: Romans (60:28:3); Matthew (99:44:12); Hebrews (128:15:3) but Revelation (82:122:83).

28 Elisabeth Schüssler Fiorenza, *The Book of Revelation: Justice and Judgement* (Philadelphia: Fortress Press, 1985), p. 135. A more radical advocate is Robert Royalty, *The Streets of Heaven: The Ideology of Wealth in the Apocalypse of John* (Macon, GA: Mercer University Press, 1998), who argues that John intends to silence every voice except his own, including the voice of Scripture.

29 Christopher Rowland, *Revelation* (London: Epworth Press, 1993). See also his book (with Judith Kovacs) on the history of interpretation of the book in the Blackwell Series: J. Kovacs and C. Rowland, *Revelation: The Apocalypse of Jesus Christ* (Oxford: Blackwell, 2004).

6 Conclusion

1 See my *Jesus and Scripture* (London: SPCK, 2010/Grand Rapids, MI: Baker Academic, 2011), pp. 79–91.

2 Thus few scholars accept the genuineness of the three quotations of Deuteronomy in the Temptation narratives (Matt. 4.1–11/Luke 4.1–13). No one was present to record them, it is hard to imagine a conversation between Jesus and the disciples along the lines of 'The devil said this but I responded' and both versions look like expansions of Mark, which only has the bare statement that Jesus 'was in the wilderness for forty days, tempted by Satan' (Mark 1.13).

3 For such an argument, see Richard T. France, *Jesus and the Old Testament: His Application of Old Testament Passages to Himself and His Mission* (London: Tyndale, 1971).

4 Revelation 22.2 seems to have the Hebrew of Ezekiel 47.12 in mind when it speaks of 'producing its fruit each month' since the LXX only has 'bringing forth the first fruit of the crop'. On the other hand, the particular expression *ha dei genesthai meta tauta* (lit. 'things which must happen after these things') in Revelation 4.1 is identical to one of the Greek versions of Daniel 2.45.

Select bibliography

General

Beale, G. K. and Carson, D. A. (eds), *Commentary on the New Testament Use of the Old Testament* (Grand Rapids: Baker Academic, 2007).

Menken, M. J. J. and Moyise, S. (eds), *Deuteronomy in the New Testament* (London and New York: T. & T. Clark, 2008).

Menken, M. J. J. and Moyise, S. (eds), *The Minor Prophets in the New Testament* (London and New York: T. & T. Clark, 2009).

Moyise, S., *Evoking Scripture: Seeing the Old Testament in the New* (London and New York: Continuum, 2008).

Moyise, S. and Menken, M. J. J. (eds), *The Psalms in the New Testament* (London and New York: T. & T. Clark, 2004).

Moyise, S. and Menken, M. J. J. (eds), *Isaiah in the New Testament* (London and New York: T. & T. Clark, 2006).

Acts

Litwak, K., *Echoes of Scripture in Luke–Acts: Telling the History of God's People Intertextually* (JSNTSup, 282; London: T. & T. Clark, 2005).

Mallen, P., *The Reading and Transformation of Isaiah in Luke–Acts* (LNTS, 367; London: T. & T. Clark, 2008).

Meek, J. A., *The Gentile Mission in Old Testament Citations in Acts* (LNTS, 385; London: T. & T. Clark, 2008).

Pao, D. W., *Acts and the Isaianic New Exodus* (WUNT, 2.130; Tübingen: Mohr Siebeck, 2000).

1/2 Peter, Jude, James

Bauckham, R. J., *Jude, 2 Peter* (WBC, 50; Waco, TX: Word, 1983).

Bauckham, R. J., *James: Wisdom of James, Disciple of Jesus the Sage* (New York: Routledge, 1999).

Donelson, L. R., *I & II Peter and Jude* (Louisville: Westminster John Knox Press, 2010).

Schutter, W. L., *Hermeneutics and Composition in 1 Peter* (WUNT 2.30; Tübingen: Mohr Siebeck, 1989).

Hebrews

Allen, D. M., *Deuteronomy and Exhortation in Hebrews* (Tübingen: Mohr Siebeck, 2007).

Docherty, S. E., *The Use of the Old Testament in Hebrews* (WUNT 2.260; Tübingen: Mohr Siebeck, 2009).

Gheorghita, R., *The Role of the Septuagint in Hebrews: An Investigation of its Influence with Special Consideration to the Use of Hab 2:3–4 in Heb 10:37–38* (WUNT 2.160; Tübingen: Mohr Siebeck, 2003).

Hughes, G. R., *Hebrews and Hermeneutics* (Cambridge: Cambridge University Press, 1979).

Human, D. J. and Steyn, G. J. (eds), *Psalms and Hebrews: Studies in Reception* (LHB, 527; New York and London: T. & T. Clark, 2010).

Revelation

Bauckham, R. J., *The Climax of Prophecy: Studies on the Book of Revelation* (Edinburgh: T. & T. Clark, 1993).

Beale, G. K., *John's Use of the Old Testament in Revelation* (JSNTSup, 166; Sheffield: Sheffield Academic Press, 1998).

Bredin, M., *Jesus, Revolutionary of Peace: A Nonviolent Christology in the Book of Revelation* (Carlisle: Paternoster, 2003).

Caird, G. B., *The Revelation of St. John the Divine* (2nd edn; London: A. & C. Black, 1984).

Kovacs, J. and Rowland, C., *Revelation: The Apocalypse of Jesus Christ* (Oxford: Blackwell, 2004).

Matthewson, D., *A New Heaven and a New Earth: The Meaning and Function of the Old Testament in Revelation 21.1—22.5* (JSNTSup, 238; Sheffield: Sheffield Academic Press, 2003).

Moyise, S. (ed.), *Studies in the Book of Revelation* (Edinburgh: T. & T. Clark, 2001).

Index of biblical references

Index of authors and subjects